P9-CCR-358

DISCARDED

Cloning

MAPLE DALE SCHOOL LIBRARY
8377 N. Port Washington Rd.
Milwaukee, Wisconsin 53217

Look for these and other books in the Lucent Overview Series:

Abortion
Alcoholism
Artificial Organs
The Brain
Cancer
Cloning
Depression
Diabetes
Drug Abuse
Eating Disorders

Epidemics
Euthanasia
Genetic Engineering
Health Care
Memory
Mental Illness
Organ Transplants
Smoking
Suicide

Cloning

by Jeanne DuPrau

Lucent
Books

MAPLE DALE SCHOOL LIBRARY
8377 N. Port Washington Rd.
Milwaukee, Wisconsin 53217

Library of Congress Cataloging-in-Publication Data

DuPrau, Jeanne.
    Cloning / by Jeanne DuPrau.
       p.   cm. — (Overview series)
    Includes bibliographical references and index.
    Summary: Discusses the methods, regulation, and ethics of cloning in relation to agriculture, medicine, endangered species, and human beings.
    ISBN 1-56006-583-4 (lib. alk. paper)
    1. Cloning Juvenile literature.   [1. Cloning.   2. Genetic engineering.]   I. Title.   II. Series: Lucent overview series.
QH442.2.D87   2000
660.6'5—dc21
                                        99-28320
                                           CIP

No part of this book may be reproduced or used in any form or by any means, electrical, mechanical, or otherwise, including, but not limited to, photocopy, recording, or any information storage and retrieval system, without prior written permission from the publisher.

Copyright © 2000 by Lucent Books, Inc.
P.O. Box 289011, San Diego, CA 92198-9011
Printed in the U.S.A.

660.6 DU

Contents

INTRODUCTION   6

CHAPTER ONE   10
Flowers, Farms, and Forests: Cloning in Agriculture

CHAPTER TWO   21
Cloning in Medicine

CHAPTER THREE   35
Cloning Endangered Species

CHAPTER FOUR   47
Cloning Human Beings

CHAPTER FIVE   60
Questions of Right and Wrong

CHAPTER SIX   76
Regulating Human Cloning

NOTES   87
GLOSSARY   92
ORGANIZATIONS TO CONTACT   94
SUGGESTIONS FOR FURTHER READING   96
WORKS CONSULTED   98
INDEX   106
PICTURE CREDITS   111
ABOUT THE AUTHOR   112

MAPLE DALE SCHOOL LIBRARY
8377 N. Port Washington Rd.
Milwaukee, Wisconsin 53217
2002529

Introduction

ON JULY 5, 1996, in a shed near the town of Roslin, Scotland, a remarkable lamb was born. The people who gathered around to observe this lamb's birth were not sheep farmers but scientists who worked at a research center called the Roslin Institute. They named the lamb Dolly.

Dolly looked quite ordinary. She had grayish white wool and weighed fourteen and a half pounds. But in a few months, she would become the world's most famous sheep. What made Dolly remarkable was that she was a clone, the first of her kind. She had not been made in the usual way—by the coming together of a male sheep and a female sheep out in the pasture. Her life began in a laboratory.

A clone is an exact genetic copy of a living thing—that is, the genes of the clone are exactly the same as the genes of the plant or animal that the clone was made from. Genes are like sets of instructions that reside in an animal's cells. These instructions tell the cell what to do. In a petunia plant, for example, the genes determine—among many other things—the shape and color of the flower, the size of the plant, and how well the plant resists diseases and insects. In a human being, the genes determine characteristics such as hair color, eye color, and height. Whether a child has a nose like its mother's or hands like its father's, whether it is going to be plump or skinny, short or tall, have straight teeth or crooked, need glasses or not—all this depends on genes. There are also some genes that cause diseases, such as cystic fibrosis or hemophilia.

It is easy to make an exact genetic copy of a plant. If, for example, a leaf from an African violet is placed in water, it will put out roots and grow into a new plant, one that has the same genes as the first plant. It has cloned itself—that is, reproduced itself without any seed or fertilization being involved. The new plant is not the product of two "parent" plants whose genes have been joined by cross-pollination. It has only one "parent," the plant from which it was cloned.

Some of the lower forms of animals also have the ability to clone themselves. One of these is the planaria worm. If you cut a planaria worm in three pieces, each of those pieces will grow into a new worm. All three will be genetically the same.

But for a long time scientists thought that higher animals, particularly mammals, could not be cloned. Their experiments appeared to have proved that it was impossible to take a cell from a grown animal—a liver cell, for instance, or a skin cell—and cause it to grow into a new animal. The scientist whose experiment produced Dolly, an embryologist named Ian Wilmut, proved them wrong.

Wilmut took some cells from the udder of an adult sheep. He figured out a way to make these cells into the kind of cells from which an animal's life begins, cells in which the genes "know how" to make the entire animal.

Some lower forms of animals, such as the planaria worm, use cloning as a means of survival.

He put the genes from one of these cells into a sheep egg whose genes had been removed. Then he gave the egg a tiny electric shock, and the egg began to divide and grow, becoming an embryo (a very early stage of life).

All this took place in the laboratory, under a microscope. But it is not possible to "grow" an entire animal in a laboratory dish. So when the embryo was still very small, Wilmut placed it inside the womb of a living sheep. The embryo developed normally, and Dolly was born.

Dolly's amazing conception stunned the scientific world and ushered in a new era of cloning—an era that is proving both revolutionary and controversial.

What made Dolly different from any sheep ever born before was that *all her genes came from one animal.* She did not have the combined genes of a mother and a father; she had only one parent, the sheep from whom the udder cells were taken.

When Dolly was announced to the world, people immediately saw exciting possibilities. If sheep could be cloned, perhaps other animals could, too. Maybe the best cows could be cloned to produce herds of excellent cows, or champion racehorses could be cloned to produce more champions. It might be possible to clone animals from endangered species to keep those species from dying out. It might even be possible to clone human beings.

But to many people, what Wilmut had done was more alarming than exciting. To make a copy of an animal in a laboratory seemed to be breaking the rules of nature. It opened the door to experiments that tinkered with the very foundations of life.

"It's unbelievable," said Lee Silver, a molecular biologist at Princeton University. "It basically means that there are no limits. It means that all of science fiction is true."[1] Science fiction, of course, can depict both bright and dark futures. Whether cloning will offer benefits or dangers—or both—to humankind, no one yet knows for sure. But people all over the world are debating the question.

1

Flowers, Farms, and Forests: Cloning in Agriculture

THE IDEA OF cloning was around long before Dolly—in fact, cloning has been done for centuries. Until fairly recently, however, all cloning was done with plants, not with animals. Cloning was a way for farmers and other plant growers to give a boost to nature and make their own jobs easier.

Cloning flowers

Plant breeders have been taking advantage of the predictability of cloning for a long time. They know they are going to get a perfect copy of the plant or animal they started with: the clone will have exactly the same genes as the original. This predictability can be a great benefit in many fields.

Consider the business of growing flowers. For example, a field of chrysanthemum plants grown from seed is vulnerable in many ways. The plants can be damaged by too much cold or heat; they can be attacked by insects; and the chrysanthemum blooms can vary in size, form, or color. The farmer who grows plants from seed never knows exactly how his crop of flowers is going to turn out.

If he grows his chrysanthemums by cloning them, however, he *does* know. He can take cells from the chrysanthemum plant he wants to reproduce, put these cells in a test tube with the nutrients the cell needs, and grow a new plant

that will be exactly the same as the one he started with. If he takes thousands of cells from that first chrysanthemum plant, he can grow thousands of new plants. Each one will produce the very same kind of chrysanthemum. This process is called tissue culture.

Plant breeders rely on tissue cultures to clone flowers like these greenhouse chrysanthemums.

In addition to giving him uniform flowers, cloning saves the chrysanthemum farmer space. It might take half an acre or so to grow a thousand chrysanthemum plants. But if he grows clones in test tubes, he can raise that many plants on a few long shelves in his greenhouse. Cloning saves time, too: plants grown in test tubes bloom sooner than plants grown from seed.

Cloning food crops

The advantages of cloning flowers also apply to food crops: by cloning the best plants, farmers can make sure their fruits, vegetables, and grains are consistently good. In the nineteenth century, growers developed an especially tasty apple called Cox's Orange Pippin. This apple tree was cloned—that is, a cutting from it was used to start a new tree—and since then, all Cox's Orange Pippin apple trees have been clones of that first tree. In the same way, all Idaho potatoes and all Red Delicious apples are clones

In Kilrush, Ireland, a poor family desperately searches for edible potatoes during the Irish Potato Famine of the 1840s.

of an original plant. So are all the navel orange trees in Southern California. In fact, the original parent of them all is still growing in Riverside, California.

There are some dangers, however, in growing crops by cloning. When all the plants are genetically the same, they will all have the same reaction to a disease. If one plant is vulnerable to a certain disease, all of them will be. A terrible example of this occurred in Ireland in the 1840s.

At that time, many of the poorest people in the country lived on potatoes—Ireland's main crop—and not much else. Because potatoes are almost always grown by cloning, when a fungus attacked Irish potato crops in 1845, all the potatoes in Ireland were susceptible to it. Potato fields were destroyed on a massive scale. More than a million people died of starvation. This disaster is known as the Irish Potato Famine.

Now farmers take precautions to protect crops of clones from disease epidemics. Instead of planting only one kind of potato or corn or wheat, they plant several varieties. A disease that affects one variety may have no effect on the others. Cloning can also be a protection against plant diseases. If a plant proves to be resistant to a certain disease, that plant can be cloned, making all the resulting plants disease resistant also.

In addition to producing more and better plants, cloning can sometimes have another benefit: it can help to protect the environment.

The case of the wild orchid

In the early nineteenth century, European explorers brought home fascinating plants from exotic lands. These plants, which had gorgeous flowers and a wonderful fragrance, were wild orchids. They were unlike anything Europeans had seen before, and they soon became tremendously popular. People who had orchid plants for sale could make a great deal of money. So collectors traveled to the forests and jungles where the orchids grew and dug them up by the thousands. Entire areas were stripped of these beautiful and delicate flowers. It was, said one English botanist in 1878, "wanton robbery."[2]

It would have been far less destructive to bring a few plants back from their native habitat and then grow more from their seeds. But this is an extremely slow process with orchids. From the cymbidium orchid, for example, a grower might get six or eight new plants over a period of ten years. But in the 1960s, it was discovered that orchids could be multiplied by cloning. The cymbidium orchid could be made to produce as many as a billion plants in only nine months. This meant a constant supply of flowers for the growers, and, most important, it meant protection for the orchids in their native habitat. Collectors could no longer make money by uprooting and bringing back thousands of plants; the European orchid breeders could clone their own.

Cloning orchids protects an important though relatively small segment of the environment. But cloning also offers hope for protecting a very large segment of the environment: the world's forests.

Cloning forests

Every year, about eight billion trees are cut down for the needs of human beings: to make paper, furniture, houses, fences. That is approximately twenty-one million trees a day. Forests are shrinking fast all over the planet. Experts warn that a way to replace them must be found—partly because people will continue to use wood and also because the carbon dioxide that trees produce is crucial to Earth's atmosphere. But over the last century or so, people have been cutting trees at a much faster rate than they can be replanted.

Cloning might solve the problem. In 1998, an Australian company called ForBio announced a new technology for cloning and growing trees.

Forestry scientists have been cloning trees for years, in much the same way that farmers clone vegetables and plant breeders clone flowers. But in this case the cloning process—making cuttings and placing them in test tubes full of nutrients—is slow and tedious. A person can produce about one thousand clonings a day. At this rate, it would be very expensive and take a very long time to produce enough trees for a commercial forest; that is, a forest of trees intended to be cut down for human use. The Australian company has speeded up the process enormously by designing robots to take over the cloning job. A robot can produce fifteen thousand clonings a day, and at this rate the company hopes to be producing fifty million trees a year by 2003.

Because the original cells are taken from the straightest, healthiest trees the researchers can find, a forest of cloned trees will look rather strange. All the trees will be of about equal size. They will all be the same age, and they will all be as straight and healthy as the "parent" tree. At harvest-time, the lumberjacks will not have to search for the best trees. They will all be equally good.

Forests of cloned trees, however, are no substitute for natural forests. The great ancient forests of the Pacific Northwest, for example, are much more than sources of wood. They are places of immense beauty and complexity, home to many varieties of plants and wildlife. Plantations of cloned trees might have a role in saving these irreplace-able forests. "The ability to engineer enormous numbers of trees for commercial use should reduce some of the pres-sure on native forests,"[3] says Bob Teasdale, one of the founders of ForBio. Lumber firms could harvest the clones and leave the ancient forests standing.

In an effort to preserve ancient forests from logging, researchers are devising new methods to speed the cloning process for trees.

Selective breeding and twinning

Now that the creation of Dolly has shown that it is possible to clone animals, animal breeders are hoping that cloning will soon provide them with the same kinds of advantages that it has offered to plant growers. Dairy farmers, for example, are among those who might benefit greatly from the technology that Ian Wilmut pioneered.

Dairy farmers will benefit from new technology that will allow their healthiest, most productive cows to be cloned.

The goal of a dairy farmer is to produce as much milk as possible for the least amount of money. To do this, the farmer needs the best possible cows—the ones that are the healthiest and give the most milk. So he works to improve and increase his herd. The most obvious way to improve the herd is simply to breed the best animals together. This is called selective breeding. The farmer chooses two animals that have all the qualities he wants. He then mates them to each other, hoping that the resulting calf will combine the best of its mother's and its father's characteristics. But he can never be sure that this will happen. Genes combine in unpredictable ways. He may get the exceptional cow he wants, and he may not.

Besides ordinary breeding, dairy farmers in recent years have used a technique called "twinning" to increase the size of their herds more quickly. Twinning is actually a kind of cloning. At a very early stage of development, a cow embryo is pinched in half, which produces identical twins. The farmer gets two calves instead of one.

A herd of champion milk cows

Neither selective breeding nor twinning can guarantee a top-quality calf. Cloning could change that. The first steps have already been taken. In 1997, a Wisconsin company called Infigen presented its first clone, a bull named Gene, and announced that it had developed a new cloning technology that would be of great help to dairy farmers. "We can make . . . identical animals possessing a desired trait,"[4] a researcher at the company said.

Companies like this would probably produce cow embryos rather than full-grown cows. A farmer could order hundreds of embryos from a catalog describing the merits of each kind. He might choose, for example, a cow known for producing large quantities of milk. When the embryos were delivered, he would place them in the wombs of the cows in his herd, where they would grow and from which they would eventually be born. Fairly quickly, a dairy farmer could end up with a herd of cows that were all genetically the same—every one of them a prize milk giver.

This would make milk production less expensive, too. To get a certain amount of milk—say, a thousand gallons—he would need fewer cows than before. Maintaining this smaller herd would cost him less money.

Catalogs of cloned animals are not likely to be available in the near future, however. Cloning technology raises many interesting possibilities, but practical problems will take a while to work out. Scientists at the Roslin Institute, where Dolly was cloned, estimate that it might be between ten and twenty years before cloning becomes a routine procedure in livestock production.

Scientists have learned how to alter the milk that a cow gives to make it more nutritious for human babies. In a process known as genetic engineering, they add a human gene to the cow's own genes to make the change in the milk. If such genetically altered cows were cloned, dairy farmers could have entire herds of cows that produced this more nutritious milk.

Disease-resistant animals

Another advantage of cloning would be to produce animals that are resistant to disease. In ordinary populations of animals, there are always some that are very vulnerable to diseases and others that are not. Cloning the resistant animals could create healthier populations.

Scientists know, however, that having large groups of genetically identical animals can be dangerous. One disease that all the animals are susceptible to can wipe out entire herds, just as the fungus wiped out the Irish potato crop. Although farmers of the future might choose to have herds made up of clones (if and when they become available), they would probably be careful to have several varieties: a hundred cows that are clones of variety A, a hundred of variety B, and so on.

Is it right to clone animals?

Although the idea of cloning farm animals offers such exciting possibilities as consistently high-quality animals and disease-resistant herds, it raises some serious questions, too.

Britt. Reprinted by permission of Copley News Service.

When Dolly the sheep was born at the Roslin Institute in Scotland, Dr. Donald Bruce, director of the Church of Scotland, was moved to think about the issues raised by the event. He wrote a paper in which he explained his thoughts. The world we see around us, he said, is full of marvelous variety. We see not just a few kinds of plants and creatures but millions of kinds. "It could be argued," he writes, "that to produce replica animals on demand would be to go against something basic and God-given about the nature of life. It reduces the living organism to a narrow blueprint."[5]

He wondered, too, whether it is right to treat animals as if they are nothing more than objects for our use. "To manipulate animals to be born, grow, and reach maturity for sale and slaughter at exactly the time we want them to suit production schedules suggests a turning [of] the animal into a mere commodity," he says. "Nature is not ours to do exactly what we like with. We too are creatures, companions with all created things."[6] It may not be good for the human spirit to stamp out identical animals in the way a factory stamps out pretzels or potato chips. Some sense of kinship with the rest of nature could easily be lost.

The cloning of animals is still in its early stages, but the technology is developing very fast. As it develops, more ideas for its use are being proposed, and those ideas in turn raise more questions. One area in which the benefits as well as the ethical questions of cloning could be immense is the field of medicine.

2

Cloning in Medicine

IAN WILMUT IS famous now as the man who cloned an adult mammal for the first time. But Wilmut did not actually set out to be the first to clone an adult mammal; he was working on cloning as a means to an end, not as an end in itself. Wilmut and his colleagues at PPL Laboratories in Roslin, Scotland, had originally intended to develop new treatments for genetic disorders in human beings. Among the disorders they were most interested in is the blood disease called hemophilia.

Hemophilia: a genetic disorder

Although the drugs that people take to treat and cure their illnesses are usually produced in laboratories, the basic ingredients of those drugs often come from nature. Penicillin is derived from a mold, for example, and aspirin comes from willow bark. Some diseases, such as hemophilia, are caused by the body's lack of one or more important substances. There are more than fifteen thousand hemophiliacs in the United States. Nearly all of them are males (females are born with hemophilia only extremely rarely).

Hemophilia is caused by a genetic defect. A hemophiliac's blood does not contain the gene that makes what is known as a clotting factor. When a healthy person bleeds, a clot forms fairly soon, and thus the bleeding stops. When a hemophiliac bleeds, the bleeding is likely to go on and on unless special action is taken.

Cuts and scratches are not the main dangers for hemophiliacs, however. If a cut is bandaged tightly, the skin heals over it and stops the bleeding. The more serious danger is internal bleeding, which happens under the skin or deep inside the body. Sometimes there is no outward sign that inner bleeding is going on. In some cases, the person might feel sluggish or strange. A bump on the head can cause bleeding into the brain. Bleeding into the joints can cause the knees or elbows to bend and stiffen permanently. Bleeding that is not stopped can be fatal.

The treatment for hemophilia is transfusion. The doctor inserts a needle into the patient's vein, and a fluid that contains the missing clotting factor flows through the needle into the bloodstream. But the effect does not last. Because the body continually makes new blood, the hemophiliac's defective blood soon replaces the transfused blood, and when he bleeds again, he will need another transfusion. Hemophiliacs may need dozens of transfusions every year.

Transfusions can keep hemophiliacs alive, but there are many problems connected with them. One is expense: it

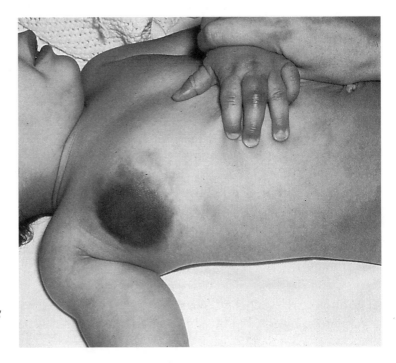

A hemophiliac baby suffers from internal bleeding. Such hemorrhages can prove fatal if hemophiliacs are unable to obtain blood transfusions containing the much-needed clotting factor.

costs between $100,000 and $200,000 to buy the clotting factor that a hemophiliac needs for one year. Another problem is a chronic shortage of blood in blood banks. Most people need blood only in emergencies, but hemophiliacs need it throughout their lives. There is never enough. The worst problem of all is the possibility of contaminated blood. Before scientists had identified the human immuno-deficiency virus that causes AIDS, a great deal of blood containing that virus ended up in blood banks. To date, more than four thousand hemophiliacs have died from AIDS as a result of contaminated transfusions. Hepatitis can also be transmitted this way, and hepatitis is the third greatest cause of death among hemophiliacs.

Hemophilia medicine through cloning

Cloning technology could make a huge difference for hemophiliacs, and this is what Ian Wilmut and his colleagues at PPL Laboratories were working on. They had found that it was possible to alter a sheep's genes so that the instruction the genes give to the cells is "don't make this particular milk protein, but instead make clotting factor VIII, which is needed for hemophilia."[7] The milk of a sheep that is altered in this way will contain the clotting factor, which can be separated from the milk and given as medicine.

Scientists were already able to do this before the cloning of Dolly, but it was not a practical way of producing large quantities of the clotting factor. Scientists had to sit for hours at their microscopes; the work was tedious and the success rate was low. But cloning techniques could change that. Once a sheep's genes had been altered to produce milk containing the clotting factor, the sheep could be cloned, producing another sheep with the same genes and, therefore, the same milk. Just a few such sheep would be enough to found a flock of identical animals, all of them making the clotting factor in their milk. "It allows us to develop products more rapidly than earlier technologies," says Ron James, PPL's managing director. "Typically, we can get products into the clinic two years sooner than before."[8]

At the Roslin Institute, scientists are researching ways to clone sheep like Dolly (right) and Polly so that their milk will produce the blood clotting factor necessary to treat hemophilia.

Treatment for other genetic diseases

The same cloning techniques that might benefit hemophilia could also be used to treat other genetic diseases, such as cystic fibrosis, which causes certain glands to secrete a sticky substance that can settle in the lungs and make breathing very difficult. People with cystic fibrosis usually do not live to be much older than thirty. Scientists at the Roslin laboratory have already altered the genes of sheep so that their milk produces a drug called alpha-1 antitrypsin, which is used to treat cystic fibrosis. If they could clone these sheep, they would produce "living drug factories" that would make the drug much more quickly and much more cheaply than can be done in a laboratory. Diabetes is another disease that cloning might benefit in the same way. The "living drug factories" could be made to produce insulin, which diabetics need.

The hope of using cloning to make medicine is close to being realized. Ian Wilmut, in a 1997 interview, said, "I think there will be animals on the ground with interesting new products in three years."[9] Other medical uses of cloning are farther off and yet intensely interesting to researchers. One of these is the idea of using animal clones to provide organs for transplanting into human beings.

Organ transplants

In 1967, Dr. Christiaan Barnard performed the first heart transplant. He took the heart from a twenty-five-year-old woman who had died in a car accident and placed it into the chest of a fifty-five-year-old man with serious heart disease. This man lived only three weeks beyond his operation, but Barnard's next transplant patient, Philip Blaiberg, lived for seventeen months. Suddenly, doctors all over the world were trying out this new kind of surgery, in the hope of saving patients with bad hearts who were otherwise doomed to die. But the technique was not a great success at first. By 1969, doctors worldwide had done 166 heart transplants, but only 23 of their patients were still alive.

The problem was not the surgery itself, as the new hearts could be sewn neatly into place and would function well. The problem was that the body of the patient perceived the new heart as a foreign invader and tried to reject it. Infections developed. Patients suffered high fevers. They had to take drugs to suppress the infections, and the drugs often had dangerous side effects.

Transplant surgery has become common now, and doctors have learned more about managing the problems of organ rejection. Three years after surgery, about 75 percent of transplant patients are still alive—but to stay alive, they have to keep

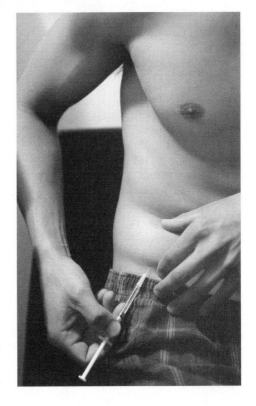

A diabetic man injects himself with insulin, another drug that scientists hope to produce through cloning techniques.

a careful watch over their health. They commonly take twenty-five or thirty pills a day, on a regular schedule. Some of these drugs weaken the immune system so that it will not fight against the new organ; others protect against the diseases that can attack people whose immune systems have been weakened. It is a delicate balance. If it tips one way, a patient's new heart or liver can be rejected. If it tips

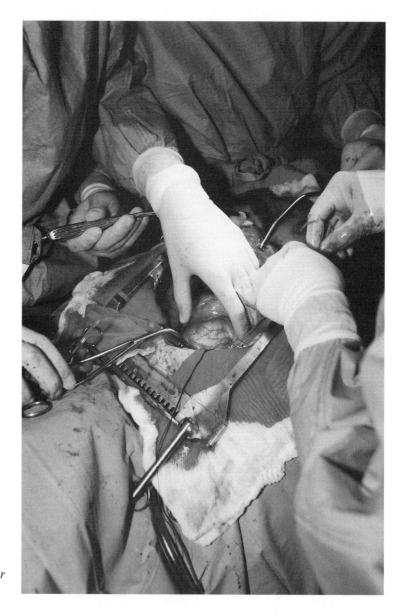

A surgeon inserts his hand into the chest cavity of a patient undergoing heart surgery. New cloning technology may increase the availability of organs and improve the success rate for heart and other organ transplants.

the other way, the patient can contract a disease such as pneumocystis, an especially dangerous form of pneumonia. Though people who would otherwise have died can gain years of quality living from organ transplants, they will be, in a very real sense, patients forever.

The other main problem with organ transplants is simply that there are not enough organs to go around. For someone with heart disease to get a new heart, someone else must die at just the right time—and the person who dies must have decided to donate his or her organ, and that organ must be the right size and the right kind for the person who needs it. Many people wait anxiously for organs to become available, and as they wait, they grow sicker. In the United States, about three thousand people die every year while waiting for the organ transplant they need.

A new kind of transplant

The new cloning and genetic technology has raised a possibility that researchers are hotly debating. They know already that human genes can be inserted into the genes of animals, in the same way that the scientists at PPL Laboratories put the gene for a human clotting factor into the genes of a sheep. It might be possible to make animals whose organs were enough like human organs so that they would not instantly be rejected. Then those animals could be cloned, producing a large and renewable supply of organs for transplant. This kind of transplant is called xenotransplant, meaning a transplant from one species to another.

It has, in fact, already been tried. In 1984, a California surgeon transplanted a baboon's heart into a baby with a heart defect. In 1995, a man infected with HIV received a transplant of bone marrow from a baboon. Neither of these transplants worked for long.

Currently, pigs are the most likely animal-to-human transplant candidates. Primates, such as baboons and chimpanzees, are a better match for human beings, but because they are wild animals it would be harder to make sure they were disease-free. Pigs are farm animals, already raised for human purposes and easily controllable.

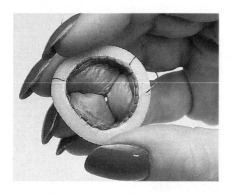

Due to medical advances, doctors are able to transplant pig organs such as this heart valve into their human patients.

Some researchers are enthusiastic about this prospect. "The goal is to ultimately replace the use of human organs with animal organs,"[10] says Dr. Joseph Tector, of the Royal Victoria Hospital in Montreal.

Potential problems

Other people, however, are more doubtful. "Xenotransplants will be rejected in a short period of time,"[11] says Dr. Malcolm Baines of McGill University. For example, he says, a pig kidney transplanted into another kind of animal will usually be rejected within forty minutes.

This is only one of the problems that animal-to-human transplants might involve. Another is the difficulty of making absolutely sure that no viruses or other disease-causing organisms are transferred to the patient along with the new organ. Some viruses that have no effect on one species have a terrible effect on another. HIV, for example, which causes AIDS in people, is harmless in monkeys. There might be such a virus in pigs that would be undetectable until it showed up in a person with a pig's kidney.

Scientists have identified thirty thousand different viruses and variations of viruses that can infect living creatures. One researcher, Dr. Frederick Murphy of the University of California at Davis, warns that it would be nearly impossible to make sure that pig organs were free of these viruses. "The system that's being put in place in this country will involve screening for the viruses that are known," he says, "but it'll also have to be a search for viruses that we don't know about. And the methods that are used in those circumstances are a lot less sensitive, a lot more shooting in the dark, than when you actually know what virus you're looking for."[12]

Another problem with transplants is expense. The human organ transplants that were done in 1994 cost nearly $3 billion. According to one estimate, this cost could rise to $20.3 billion if every patient who needed an organ transplant received an animal's organ. Some people question whether the money it would take to genetically alter, clone, and raise the animals, ensure that the animals were free of disease, and perform the transplants would not be better spent on finding new ways to treat diseased organs and ways of preventing them in the first place.

Another objection to using animals for transplants comes from those who see this as an abuse of the animals themselves. It would not be right, they say, to raise living creatures to be nothing but "spare parts" for human beings. Alan H. Berger, executive director of the Animal Protection Institute of America, points out that the American public feels increasingly concerned about the rights of animals. "In an Associated Press poll taken in November 1995," he says, "67% of those polled agreed somewhat or strongly that an animal's right to live free of suffering should be as important as a person's right to live free of suffering. Only 8% felt that it was always right to use animals to test medical treatment; 29% felt it was never or seldom right; and 62% said it was right under some circumstances. The research community should pay attention as these opinions to protect animals have been getting stronger each year."[13]

There is another way, however, in which cloning could help people whose organs need repair or replacement, and this way does not make use of animals at all.

Growing human tissue

One of the most recent discoveries to emerge from Wilmut's research is that most of the cells in the human body can be made to clone themselves. Just as a scientist can take a few cells from a carrot and cause them to grow into a new carrot plant, so it is possible to take cells from different parts of the human body and treat them in such a way that they begin to multiply and produce new tissue.

This procedure has intriguing possibilities. One of them is a treatment for leukemia, a usually fatal disease in which a person has too many white blood cells. Blood cells are manufactured in the bone marrow, the substance inside bones. The treatment for leukemia—a drastic treatment, and the only one that is sometimes effective—is to remove all the patient's bone marrow and replace it with healthy bone marrow. The main problem is finding bone marrow that is a perfect match for the patient. This can be extremely expensive as well as difficult. A man named Jay Feinberg, for example, spent $2 million conducting a worldwide search for a donor. He searched through a pool of more than a million people before he found the single individual whose bone marrow matched his.

Cloning might eliminate the need for desperate searches like Feinberg's. Scientists could take a few cells from a leukemia patient—these might be skin cells or any other kind—and using the techniques of cloning, reprogram these cells to become bone marrow cells. Then they could grow new bone marrow that would be an exact match for the patient's.

Creating human tissue by cloning human cells could be useful in other ways as well. For example, if there are unburned areas on the body of a burn victim, surgeons can take skin from these areas and use it to graft skin to wounded areas. However, this process leaves behind a wound and a scar. If it were possible to grow new skin by cloning just a few of the patient's cells, a great deal of pain might be avoided.

Possibilities for the future

British scientists have proposed the possibility of making a "body repair kit." They foresee a time when a few cells will be taken from every newborn child. These cells will be frozen and placed in a national tissue bank, so that if that child should ever need, for instance, a skin graft, a bone marrow replacement, or even a new liver, his or her own cells could be used to create it.

Of course, this plan is still just an idea. No one has actually grown a human liver or heart or any other organ from a few human cells. But the more scientists understand how cells and genes work, the more likely it is that such an idea could become reality.

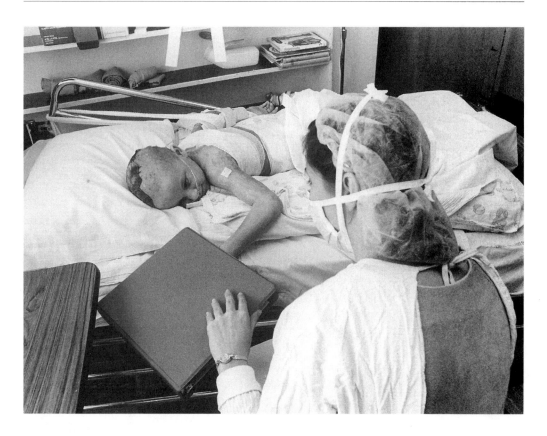

All medical advances—and especially those that venture far into unknown territory—require years of research. It is very likely that cloning will be a helpful part of that research.

Cloning as an aid to research

Animals have been used for a long time to help researchers study human diseases. But cloning could make some improvements in research efficiency.

One of the problems with conducting tests on animals is that the animals are all slightly different from each other. For example, in a group of one hundred mice, all of the same kind, each mouse has had different parents; that is, each mouse has genes that have combined in ways slightly different from all the other mice. So when a scientist does a test on this group of mice, there will be variations in the way the mice react. The scientist cannot be absolutely sure

Medical researchers hope to master the ability to clone human cells and thereby grow human tissue, which would be a boon for burn victims in need of skin grafts.

whether the results have to do with the test itself or with individual differences between the mice. He has to use a large number of mice in order to see an overall trend.

If that scientist were using cloned mice, however, genetic differences would not be a problem. All the mice would be identical. He would need fewer mice for his experiments, and he would know that whatever variations he saw were not the result of a genetic difference.

Because it is possible now to add and subtract genes from animals' cells, researchers could create animals that have the genes for a specific genetic disease. They could make, for example, a sheep with cystic fibrosis, then clone that sheep to produce models of the disease for research. This might be a way to learn more about such diseases and how to treat them.

But it also raises the same kinds of ethical questions as cloning animals for organ transplants: is it right to make

Animal rights activists protest the use of animals in scientific experiments, condemning the practice as both inhumane and ineffective.

animals suffer for human purposes or to purposely create an animal that has a painful and fatal disease? These questions would have to be debated before such experimentation could proceed. On one side of the debate would be those who believe that the human benefit justifies the animal's suffering. The Foundation for Biomedical Research, for instance, believes that it is absolutely necessary to use animals in medical research. "Nearly every major medical advance of the 20th century has depended largely on research with animals," their statement says. "Our best hope for developing preventions, treatments and cures for diseases such as Alzheimer's, AIDS, and cancer will also involve biomedical research using animals."[14] This organization emphasizes the importance of taking good care of the animals used for research, to make sure that their suffering is minimized.

On the other side are those who do not believe that animals should be made to suffer for human purposes and who advocate other methods of research. The organization called People for the Ethical Treatment of Animals (PETA) points out that other ways of conducting medical research are not only more humane but more effective than experimenting on animals. "Human clinical and epidemiological studies, cadavers, and computer simulators are faster, more reliable, less expensive, and more humane than animal tests," says a PETA spokesperson. "Ingenious scientists have developed, from human brain cells, a model 'microbrain' with which to study tumors, as well as artificial skin and bone marrow. We can now test irritancy on egg membranes, produce vaccines from cell cultures, and perform pregnancy tests using blood samples instead of killing rabbits."[15] According to this point of view, it is possible to have it all—research that is both effective and humane.

A new world of information

Perhaps the most useful way cloning can help medical research is by giving scientists new insights about how genes and cells work. The discoveries made by Wilmut and others have turned old ideas upside down. That an entire animal can be grown from the cells of an adult and that cells can be reprogrammed to produce different kinds of body tissue were only recently considered impossibilities. Cloning technology has given scientists new tools for understanding how human beings work, how they stay healthy and get sick, how they grow and age. "Now," says Ian Wilmut, "people will have to think in slightly different ways about the mechanisms that control these changes—for example about what happens when things go wrong and you get a cancer instead of a normal development."[16]

Cloning has the potential to benefit human health directly in a great variety of ways. It may also help to improve human health indirectly by coming to the aid of the increasingly endangered planet on which human beings live.

3

Cloning Endangered Species

IN MOST PLACES in the world, the human population is growing, and people are building on land that was previously wilderness or countryside. As human development expands, space for other kinds of animals shrinks. Sometimes it shrinks so much that there is no place left for them to live.

This is what happened to the dusky seaside sparrow, a bird of the Florida marshlands. In the middle years of the twentieth century, as the marshes were flooded for mosquito control and filled in for buildings, the sparrow's numbers went steadily down. Finally birdwatchers could count only six—all males. One of these was captured and put in a cage at Walt Disney World, where it died on June 16, 1987. With its death, the dusky seaside sparrow became extinct.

Extinction—natural and unnatural

Extinction is not a new phenomenon. A species has a lifespan, just as an individual creature does. Throughout the 3.8-billion-year history of life on earth, species have arisen and become extinct at a fairly regular rate. Those who have studied extinction estimate that a particular species may be likely to go on for anywhere from a million to 10 million years. Then, for reasons that are sometimes well understood and sometimes mysterious, it dies out.

But by the end of the twentieth century, extinctions were occurring at an extremely high rate. Peter Raven, who is the director of the Missouri Botanical Garden, estimates that every day, about a hundred species become extinct— approximately one every fifteen minutes. Another scientist warns that at the present rate, about half of all the species on earth will be either extinct or endangered by the year 2050.

Whether a sandy beach or a rocky mountain, each habitat supports a unique ecosystem dependent on biodiversity.

It may not seem important that a little brown bird that most people have never seen or heard of vanishes from the earth. But every time a species dies, whether it is a species of bird or plant, mammal or insect, the biodiversity of the earth is diminished. The word *biodiversity* has to do with the vast number of different kinds of living things that

form an interconnected web of life all over the planet, from ocean to mountain to desert. The connections are immensely complex. The loss of one species of insect, for instance, can affect the fish that feed on that insect, which in turn might affect the birds that feed on those fish, and the ecology of an entire river might be changed. No one understands all the intricate, complex connections among the millions of species on earth. But it is certain that the destruction of any one species can ultimately endanger all the rest, and that the richness and vigor of life on earth depends on its diversity.

Could cloning preserve species?

Some researchers believe that cloning could be a way to save species that are on the brink of extinction. Perhaps if scientists had known about cloning technology before 1987, they could have taken a few cells from the skin of a dusky seaside sparrow and produced a clone—or, better yet, several clones, who could then be the start of a new flock. In fact, one such last-minute save has already been done. It happened in 1998, in New Zealand: scientists made a clone of the last of a rare breed of cow.

The New Zealand cattle

About 150 years ago, a small group of cattle ranchers attempted to establish a ranch on Enderby Island, a cold and barren bit of land near New Zealand. The ranch did not last long. The people who ran it could not tolerate the harsh conditions on the island, and they left. But the cattle managed to survive and even thrive. They adapted to a diet consisting mainly of seaweed, and over the next century their bodies changed as well: they became long in the trunk and short in the legs. By 1992, there were so many of these cattle that they were upsetting the natural ecology of the island. The government of New Zealand ordered that the herd be destroyed.

One of the breed was saved, however—a cow named Lady. She was brought back to the mainland of New Zealand and became the basis of an experiment in cloning.

To save a rare breed of cattle from extinction, researchers in New Zealand cloned cells from Lady (pictured), the only cow to be saved from the slaughter on Enderby Island.

Scientists took some cells from Lady's ovaries and caused them to form embryos, using a procedure similar to the one Ian Wilmut had used to create Dolly. They implanted each embryo into the womb of an Angus cow, and on July 1, 1998, the first calf was born.

The cloning of the New Zealand cow showed that this new technology might play an important part in saving endangered species. Scientists in a number of other places have begun to consider it.

The giant panda

One of the most endangered animals on earth is the giant panda, which lives in bamboo forests in China. It is estimated that only about one thousand pandas remain in the wild, along with about one hundred in captivity, in zoos and research centers. Over the years people have tried very hard to get pandas to breed in captivity, but it does not often happen. In 1996, eight pandas were born in captivity, but only three of them survived. Even in the wild, pandas do not produce many offspring. They are very solitary creatures and seem to be extremely picky with regard to a mate.

Chinese scientists are looking seriously at the possibility of cloning as a way to preserve the panda. They hope to achieve this feat within five years. First, however, they will have to overcome some major problems.

Despite efforts to breed giant pandas in captivity, the species stands on the brink of extinction.

Scientists can easily take from a panda's ear a bit of skin containing hundreds of cells, each of which contains the genetic material for producing a complete new panda; in theory, several hundred pandas could be cloned from these cells. But the genes from each cell must be injected into panda eggs before they can begin to turn into embryos. It is hard to obtain the eggs of a mammal without harming the animal—and of course no one wants to take the risk of harming a panda.

Even supposing scientists succeeded in growing embryos, they would soon face another problem. When an embryo gets to a certain size, it needs a female panda to grow in. But there are not enough pandas for this to be possible. So few pandas are in existence that no one is willing to experiment with them in this manner, even if they could capture and keep enough of them in the first place.

It has occurred to the Chinese researchers tackling this problem that they might put the panda embryo into the womb of a closely related species, just as the embryo of the Enderby Island cow was put into the womb of an Angus cow. The trouble is that no one is sure what animal—if any—is most closely related to the panda. "For years there's been this debate among taxonomists [scientists who classify living things] whether pandas are more closely related to raccoons or bears," says Betsy Dresser, who directs the Audubon Center for Research on Endangered Species. "And the world of science has never really determined an answer, so it's anybody's guess."[17] This means that even if the scientists could produce a panda embryo, they might have nowhere to put it. It might not survive or grow properly in either a raccoon or a bear.

Experiments are under way with other animals, however, in an effort to prove that it may be possible, at least in some cases, to use one species to carry the clone of another.

All-purpose cow eggs

Until recently, scientists were fairly sure that if you took genetic material (DNA) from, say, a pig and placed it into the egg of a cow (from which the cow genes had been removed), nothing would happen—that the pig genes and the cow egg would be incompatible. But researchers in Wisconsin have discovered that this is not entirely true. They put genes from sheep, pigs, rats, and monkeys into cow eggs and found that the eggs began to divide and form embryos—not cow embryos, and not half-cow-half-something-else embryos, but the embryo of the animal whose genes they had used. It seemed that the cow egg was serving as a place for the embryo to grow—that with its genes removed, the egg was not specifically "cow" any more, but could accommodate and nurture the genes of other kinds of animals. If this technique turned out to be practical, it might provide a solution for the Chinese scientists working to save the giant panda.

Experiments with cow eggs are still in the early stages. So far, only embryos have been produced, no full-grown live animals. "The results look encouraging," said Tanja Dominko, a researcher who worked on the project. "But at this point we have many more questions than we have answers."[18] No one yet knows whether it would be possible to grow, for instance, a sheep embryo from a cow's egg, implant it into a cow's womb, and expect the cow to give birth to a lamb. Such an idea seems stranger than fiction, yet some people are proposing ideas that seem stranger still.

Back from extinction?

In 1983, a group of scientists got together to talk about retrieving genetic material (DNA) from insects and animals that had become extinct long ago. Their purpose was to use this DNA to study these ancient animals and learn more about evolution. But they discussed other ideas as well. In a newsletter published by this group, a scientist named Jack Tkach wrote:

> Somewhere there may be a mosquito that fed on a dinosaur and got preserved in amber. If one could recover a white blood cell of a dinosaur from the stomach of a mosquito, he might be able to transplant it into an enucleated egg [an egg with the nucleus removed] and grow dinosaur tissue culture or ultimately a dinosaur.[19]

This was the idea on which the movie *Jurassic Park* was based. The movie was fiction, but there is a germ of truth at the heart of it. Scientists know now that the DNA in most of an animal's cells contains instructions that can be used to grow an entire new animal. They have also discovered that they can retrieve DNA from the remains of animals that died thousands or even millions of years ago, if, for instance, the animal's body has been frozen for all that time or if an insect has been preserved in amber. The DNA of these ancient animals—such as the dinosaur, the woolly mammoth, and the saber-toothed tiger—might be a sort of tool kit for reconstructing vanished creatures.

Through cloning, scientists may eventually be able to create and study living dinosaurs, moving scientific research from mere models to actual life forms.

Of course, all the problems that go with cloning living animals would first have to be solved. It would not be easy to find an animal that could carry a dinosaur embryo and

give birth to a baby dinosaur. So bringing back extinct species remains a fantasy at this point. But it is possible that scientists of the future will figure out how to do it.

One thing is certain: many animal species will vanish forever unless people can find ways to save them. Although cloning to save endangered species is, for the most part, just an idea, there are preparations under way that might give it a boost if and when it becomes possible.

Tissue banks

At the University of Alaska Museum in Fairbanks, in two large and extremely cold freezers, is a collection of twenty-three thousand animals. These are not whole animals, of course. They are samples of animal tissue, a small number of cells from each kind of animal, frozen in vials. The university began this collection in 1991. The purpose of the Alaska Frozen Tissue Collection, as it is called, is to help scientists study species' genetic makeup, the diseases that affect them, and how they evolve over time. But these tissue samples might also be important for learning about and helping to save endangered species. When scientists learn more about cloning, they might be able to use these tissue samples as the basis for new animals.

There is a similar collection at the San Diego Zoo, in the Center for Reproduction of Endangered Species. Since the late 1970s, researchers there have been collecting genetic samples from rare animals that may eventually become extinct. Their cells, safely frozen and stored, are a kind of insurance policy against permanent loss.

It is not at all certain, however, that cloning will be the answer—in whole or in part—to the problem of vanishing species. A great many problems remain, and there is no guarantee that they can be solved.

Preserving genetic diversity

Suppose that all the technical problems of cloning were solved, and that scientists could take cells from, say, a panda, grow a thousand panda embryos, place them into

A geneticist at the San Diego Zoo's Center for Reproduction of Endangered Species displays vials containing the frozen tissue samples of rare animals.

the wombs of bears, and produce a thousand new pandas to go out into the bamboo forests. This sounds like a good idea, but it might not be. All the cloned pandas would be genetically identical. Whatever baby pandas they produced would be genetically identical to their parents. There would be no genetic diversity in a population of cloned pandas, and, as previously noted, the lack of genetic diversity can be perilous.

The same dangers apply to a group of genetically identical animals as to a field of genetically identical plants, such as the potatoes that succumbed to blight during the Irish Potato Famine. In an ordinary population of animals, every individual is slightly different from every other; some would probably be able to resist a given disease and survive. But in a population of clones, all the individuals are equally susceptible to whatever germ comes along. An entire group of panda clones could be wiped out by one disease.

Another reason for preserving genetic diversity is to allow for useful changes to take place over the years. Every time two animals mate, their genes combine in unpredictable ways. This means that occasionally an animal is born with a useful new characteristic—maybe a thicker coat that enables it to withstand cold; maybe a better sense of smell that helps it find food; maybe longer legs or stronger muscles. Changes such as these can then be passed on as that animal finds mates, and the condition of the flock as a whole can change and improve. With cloned animals, such changes would not happen.

The root of the problem

The main reason why many scientists doubt that cloning is the answer for saving endangered species is that cloning does not go to the root of the problem. If a thousand

If these cubs were clones—rather than the natural offspring—of this female cheetah, they would lack the genetic diversity necessary for producing evolutionary changes within their species.

MAPLE DALE SCHOOL LIBRARY
8377 N. Port Washington Rd.
Milwaukee, Wisconsin 53217

Florida panthers could be cloned and then set free to roam the Florida swamps again, they would run into the same problems that caused them to become endangered in the first place—the encroachment of human beings into their habitat.

This is why some scientists and organizations are not interested in cloning as a way to preserve species. "We're not concerned with stopping species from going extinct," says Rodger Schlickeisen, president of Defenders of Wildlife, "but with curbing the rate [of extinction], which is thousands of times more than the natural rate."[20] Habitat preservation is crucial to that effort. Air and water pollution from cars and industries, highways that pave over fields, overlogging of forests, and oil spills in the ocean are each examples of the ways in which people damage and destroy areas that nurture the life of the planet. As these places vanish, animals vanish, too.

It may turn out that cloning is a partial answer. In the case of the giant panda, for instance, or other animals whose kind has dwindled down to just a few individuals, it could be a good idea to clone that last one to keep the species from blinking out forever. Cloning might be a way to buy time—the time it will take to restore animal habitats and to learn to save them from destruction in the future.

4

Cloning Human Beings

WHEN THE CLONING of Dolly the sheep was announced to the world, a new question arose in people's minds: If it is true after all that an adult mammal can be cloned, does this mean that human beings, too, can be cloned?

The answer, according to many scientists, is probably yes. "There is no reason in principle why you couldn't do it,"[21] says Ian Wilmut, the scientist who cloned Dolly. But scientists attempting to clone human beings would encounter some problems that Ian Wilmut did not have to deal with.

The basic steps

Ian Wilmut started his cloning experiment with udder cells from one sheep and an egg (with its genetic material removed) from another sheep. He put the genetic material from the cells into the egg, gave the egg a small jolt of electricity, and it began to divide and become an embryo.

The cloning of a human being could begin the same way. An egg would be taken from a woman's ovary and its genetic material removed. Cells would be taken from the person to be cloned, and genetic material from one of these cells would be injected into the egg. If all went well, a human embryo would begin to grow in a dish in a laboratory. After a few days, this embryo would be implanted in a woman's uterus to grow into a baby and eventually be born.

The failure rate

In cloning a person there would be problems that were nonexistent in the case of cloning a sheep. One problem is simply that scientists are reluctant to take the same kinds of risks with a person as with an animal. When Wilmut began his experiment, he was not at all sure whether it would work, and, for the most part, it did not.

Wilmut began his experiment with 277 udder cells and as many sheep eggs. Using the genetic material from the udder cells, he attempted to make embryos that would divide and grow. This is not an easy process, as sometimes the new genes take effect and other times they do not. Wilmut managed to make twenty-nine embryos, which were transferred into the wombs of sheep in the hope that they would grow normally and become lambs. But most of the pregnancies resulted in miscarriages. Only one of the embryos created from the udder cells developed into a lamb and was born. That one was Dolly.

Out of 277 tries, Wilmut had one success. This low rate of success has also been true of cloning attempts that have occurred after that of Dolly's, although as scientists learn more, the success rate rises. A scientist who cloned two monkeys did so after 166 unsuccessful tries. Scientists in Japan placed two cloned calf embryos in each of five cows, hoping that each cow would have twins. Out of these 10 attempts, eight calves were born—an 80 percent success rate. Nevertheless, the risk of failure is still thought too great for cloning to be tried on human beings. A woman trying to have a cloned child might have to undergo many miscarriages before bearing a live baby. More than likely, no researcher would conduct an experiment with such a high probability of causing pain and emotional distress.

Risk to the child?

Some scientists assert that cloning could result in deformed or otherwise defective babies. One unsettling piece of evidence that this might indeed be a risk is something Ian Wilmut himself has observed in experiments he has done

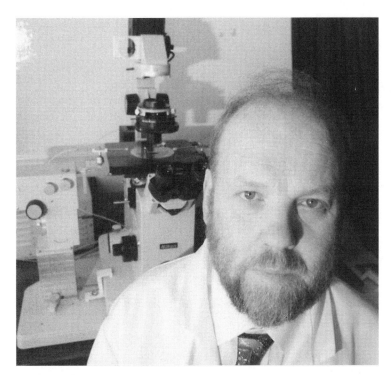

In the wake of Dolly's birth, renowned embryologist Ian Wilmut remains on the cutting edge of cloning technology.

since the birth of Dolly. Some of the lambs produced by cloning have turned out to be much larger than normal—so large that they cannot be born in the usual way but must be taken from their mothers by surgery. No one is as yet sure if this problem is related to the cloning process, but that link would have to be determined with certainty and the problem solved before cloning would be considered safe for human beings.

On the other hand, some scientists point out that cloning is actually a *less* risky way for a baby to come into being than through ordinary sexual reproduction. When a baby is conceived in the usual way, the genes of the mother and the father combine in unpredictable ways. There is always some risk that a baby will not be perfect. In fact, it is very common for abnormalities to occur, according to scientists who study human fertility. When this happens—when an embryo is produced that has the wrong number of chromosomes, for example—the woman usually has a miscarriage, often before she is aware that she is pregnant.

Sometimes a child is born with an abnormality such as Down's syndrome, which is the result of having one chromosome too many.

In a baby produced by cloning, however, such unpredictability will not occur. All the genes would come from one person, a grown person without genetic defects. So the risk of genetic abnormalities, at least, would be less than with ordinary reproduction.

No one knows, at this point, what other kinds of risks might be involved in cloning a human being. "Think of current cloning technology along the lines of the Wright brothers' first airplane flight," says Arthur Caplan of the Center for Bioethics at the University of Pennsylvania. "Many argued that human beings would never fly in a machine. The Wright brothers proved them wrong. But it took many years before the first safe, reliable and practical aircraft was up in the air."[22]

How close is human cloning?

On December 5, 1997, a scientist named Richard Seed announced that he intended to clone a person within two and a half years. He had clients already, he said: four couples who had volunteered for his project, as well as doctors who had agreed to work with him. His plan, he claimed, was to set up cloning clinics in the United States and other countries and eventually produce 200,000 clones a year at a price of less than a million dollars each.

This announcement was greeted with skepticism and disapproval by the scientific community. The safety of the technology is one concern among many. Cloning has not yet been proven safe for use on humans, and the suggestion of such a use leads to much debate over ethics. "The idea that this technology could be used in humans would be grossly unethical,"[23] said Harry Griffin, assistant director of the Roslin Institute.

Richard Seed was not discouraged by these criticisms. "There were an awful lot of people against the automobile, too," he said. "Any new technology creates fear and horror."[24]

A more credible step toward human cloning was made in December 1998, when a South Korean team of researchers announced that they had succeeded in cloning a human embryo. They grew the embryo only to a very early stage, but their experiment seems to indicate that the technology can work for human beings.

Another discovery that may assist human cloning was made at a research center in Worcester, Massachusetts, where scientists have found that cow eggs can be used to grow embryos of other species—goats, pigs, and monkeys, for example. They have used this technique to fuse a human skin cell with a cow's egg and grow human embryos. This method would solve one of the problems of the cloning process, which is the difficulty of obtaining a woman's eggs. To produce enough for experimentation,

After announcing plans to clone a human, scientist Richard Seed is interviewed by members of the press outside of his home in Riverside, Illinois.

the woman must undergo hormone treatments, and she must also have minor surgery when the doctor extracts the eggs. If cow eggs would work as well as human eggs, women would be spared considerable discomfort.

No human clone has yet been born. But it is quite possible that some day, if technical, ethical, and legal problems can be solved, one will be. What might that person be like?

Portrait of a human clone

Imagine that the first human clone, a boy, has just been born. This baby began his life under a microscope, where genes from one of his father's skin cells were injected into one of his mother's eggs, from which the genes had been removed. After the embryo had grown to a certain size in a laboratory dish, it was placed in his mother's uterus, and nine months later, the child was born. He would probably be a healthy baby who looked no different from babies conceived in the usual way.

Reprinted by permission of Ed Gamble.

What makes him different is that instead of getting half his genes from his father and half from his mother, he got *all* his genes from his father. His mother is the one who carried him and gave birth to him, but she is not genetically related to him. Genetically, this baby is like an identical twin to his father—except that he is much younger.

The father's genes, of course, come from *his* mother and father, the new baby's grandparents. Because the baby has exactly the same genes as his father, his *genetic* parents are the same as his father's. That is, his grandparents are, in a certain sense, his parents: half his genes come from his grandmother and half from his grandfather.

As the child grows, he will probably look very much the same as his father did at his age. He will have the same hair and eye color, the same body type, the same facial features. His voice will sound like his father's, and he may like to do the same things that his father did as a child. But he will not be exactly the same as his father. There will always be many differences between them.

A clone but not a carbon copy

There is one way in which this cloned child would not be an absolutely exact genetic copy of his father. Even though the genes in his mother's egg were removed and replaced with his father's genes, a tiny amount of genetic material always remains in the fluid of the egg. This is called mitochondrial DNA, and it has some influence on the genetic development of the embryo. The fact that the father and son developed in different mothers will have a small effect on their genetic makeup.

The main thing that would make this cloned child different from his father, however, is that he will grow up in a different world from the one his father grew up in. He is living at a different time, in a different place, with different people. According to the many studies that have been done on the subject, the environment in which a child lives has as much or even more influence on how that child develops than does genetics.

The child's experiences will shape him, too. He might, for instance, have a beloved dog that makes him a lifelong dog lover, whereas his father was chased by a dog at six and ever after afraid of them. His parents might be divorced when he is ten, forcing him to deal with grief and conflict in a way his father never had to. He might have a teacher in high school who encourages his interest in science, whereas his father had no such teacher and never developed his scientific aptitude, becoming a businessman instead.

No person, even a clone, is ever an exact copy of another person. Even identical twins, who are genetically the same and who grow up in the same household, become different individuals. The Dionne quintuplets, five genetically identical girls born to a Canadian family in 1934, are a striking example of this. They were a sensation, at the time. Everything possible was done to reinforce their sameness: they were dressed the same way, their hair was combed the same way, and they were even displayed to the public as if they were a sideshow. It is hard to imagine how five sisters could have a more uniform upbringing. And yet they did not have identical personalities or lead identical lives at all. Some married, some did not. One became a nun. Two became nurses. One died at the age of twenty, another at thirty-six, and the others, aged sixty-three in 1997, are still alive.

A brain cannot be cloned

George Johnson, a science writer for the *New York Times,* explains one of the main reasons why identical genes do not make identical persons: "Two genetically identical twins inside a womb will unfold in slightly different ways. The shape of the kidneys or the curve of the skull won't be quite the same. The differences are small enough that an organ from one twin can probably be transplanted into the other. But with the organs called brains the differences become profound."[25]

It is the brain that makes people who they are. As soon as a child is born, its experiences—the sound of its

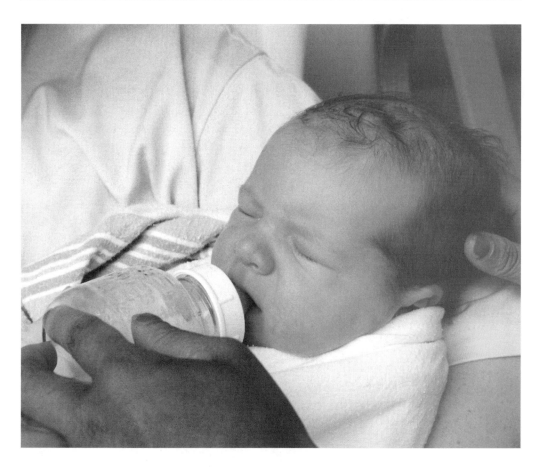

mother's voice, the prick of a diaper pin, the light from a window, a jingling toy—begin to shape its brain. Sensations such as a startling noise or the soft feel of a stuffed animal actually create new patterns in the child's brain cells, and as such experiences multiply, the brain develops into a unique and incredibly complex network of connections. Because no two people have identical experiences, no two brains are ever alike; therefore, no two people are alike.

All newborns have unique experiences that shape their lives and brain development. Thus, while a human clone would have the same genetic makeup as its "parent," its environment—and therefore its personality— would be different.

To all outward appearances, then, a clone would be the same as any other child: simply a person, with his own interests and aptitudes and his own personality. As he grew older, his personality would probably become more and more unlike his father's. There would be no doubt that he was completely himself.

Misconceptions about human cloning

One of the most common notions about cloning is that it could be used to duplicate exceptional artists, leaders, sports stars, or scientists. But once it is understood that clones are not exact copies, it is clear that this notion is false. Even if it really were possible to clone Mother Teresa or Michael Jordan, it still would not be possible to know for certain that the cloned Mother Teresa would grow up to have any interest in being a nun or if the cloned Michael Jordan would grow up to be a terrific basketball player. There are just too many other influences besides a person's genes that determine what that person will be like.

Cloning sports stars and movie stars might be pointless, anyway. What made someone like Marilyn Monroe a star in the first place was her exceptional beauty and personality. If there had been ten Marilyn Monroes, all with the same beauty and personality, none of them would have been very special. If ten Michael Jordans played basketball against each other, the game might not be very interesting.

If human cloning does become possible, people will not do it to make duplicates of famous people. They will do it for a variety of quite different reasons.

Why clone human beings?

Probably the people most interested in human cloning would be couples who want a child and for one reason or another are unable to have one in the usual way. This is a fairly common problem, and there are fertility clinics all over the country that help such couples. Often the solution is *in vitro* (in glass) fertilization—that is, the woman's egg and the man's sperm are joined in a test tube rather than inside the woman's body, and the embryo begins to grow there before it is put back into the mother's womb. But this procedure does not work for everyone. There are cases in which the man's sperm or the woman's eggs are defective or nonexistent. Such a couple cannot create a child by combining their genes. If it is the man who is infertile, the woman might have a child by using the sperm of an anonymous donor. But if cloning were an option, she might choose to carry a baby that is a clone of her husband rather than take a chance on the genes of a stranger.

Cloning might also be a solution when the mother or the father (or both) carries a gene for a disease or defect. Suppose, for instance, that the woman knows she is a carrier of the gene for hemophilia. If she and her husband have a child, there is a chance that their child would be born with the disease. They might instead decide to try cloning the husband, who would be sure to be free of the disease.

In 1988, a California couple named Abe and Mary Ayala learned that their sixteen-year-old daughter had leukemia. The doctors gave her about five years to live—unless she had a bone marrow transplant. But finding a donor whose bone marrow would match their daughter's could mean a

During a 1991 press conference at City of Hope Hospital in Duarte, California, Abe and Mary Ayala (left and center), along with their fourteen-month-old daughter, discuss the success of their elder daughter's bone marrow transplant.

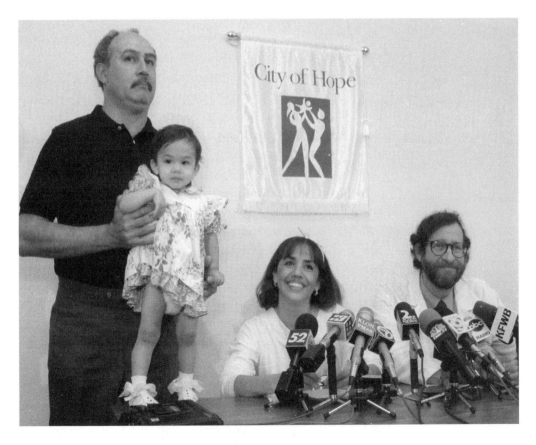

long and possibly futile search. So the Ayalas tried a drastic experiment: they conceived another child, hoping that the baby's bone marrow would be a match for that of their sick daughter. Nine months later, the new baby was born, her bone marrow *was* a match, and the transplant was made.

This kind of situation might be played out in a somewhat different way if human cloning were available. Instead of having another baby in the usual way and hoping for a match, a couple in the Ayalas' position might choose to clone their daughter, taking the genes from one of her cells and inserting them in one of the mother's eggs. The bone marrow of a child born this way would be guaranteed to be a perfect match. This would be a controversial action, however; many thinkers question whether it would be right to create a child for the sole purpose of saving another child. Any human being brought into the world, they say, should be valued for its own sake and not for someone else's purposes.

Other reasons for cloning a child

Some people have speculated that cloning might be used to replace a person who has died. If a child has a serious accident, for instance, and is in a coma and close to death, the grieving parents might take a few skin cells from that child and try to clone another child to replace the one they have lost. They might also feel that this was a way to give the child who died young another chance at life.

Still another reason for cloning a human being is suggested by Richard Dawkins, a professor at Oxford University in England, who wrote that he would love to be cloned just out of curiosity. "I find it a personally riveting thought," he said, "that I could watch a small copy of myself, 50 years younger."[26] It is doubtful that anyone would actually go to the trouble of cloning himself just out of curiosity. But someone who has an exaggerated idea of his own good qualities—someone who considers himself so superior that he believes the world needs more than one of him—might want to do so out of pure ego.

Right now, it seems fairly certain that eventually, for one reason or another, a human being will be cloned. It may be only to prove that it can be done. Some scientists believe that it will be ten years or more before the first human being is cloned. Others predict that it could be much sooner. In the meantime there continues a furious debate—not about whether human beings *can* be cloned, but whether they *should* be.

5

Questions of Right and Wrong

THE CONTROVERSY ABOUT the ethics of human cloning draws strong opinions from both sides. At one extreme are those who think it should never be done, under any circumstances. "I can't think of a morally acceptable reason to clone a human being,"[27] says Richard Mc-Cormick, a Jesuit priest and professor at the University of Notre Dame.

On the other side of the question are people such as Gregory Pence, a professor of philosophy at the University of Alabama. He can think of many reasons to clone a human being, and he sees nothing wrong with most of them. "If no one is harmed by [cloning]," he says, "then it raises no moral issue."[28]

In between these two poles is a wide-ranging argument that sometimes arouses vehement feelings in its participants. Some, such as Leon Kass, of the University of Chicago, believe that human cloning raises moral questions that are unprecedented and momentous. "We must rise to the occasion and make our judgments as if the future of our humanity hangs in the balance," he says. "For it does."[29] The International Academy of Humanism, on the other hand, has released a statement that says, "The moral issues raised by cloning are neither larger nor more profound than the questions human beings have already faced. . . . They are simply new."[30]

Whether the questions are great or small, most people agree that human cloning does present a dilemma to be wrestled with and which can be summarized as follows: Assuming that technology makes it possible, would it be morally right to clone a human being?

The dream of human betterment

One prospect that makes the idea of human cloning so intriguing is the possibility of creating human beings to order, instead of leaving it to chance, and using that power to make better people. If the most excellent specimens of humanity were cloned—those who were healthy, good looking, intelligent, and free of genetic flaws—then the number of excellent people would be increased, and, in the long run, the human race would be improved.

This might sound like a noble idea. What could be wrong with an effort to give human beings the finest possible characteristics? The trouble is that someone would have to decide what those characteristics were.

In Germany, in the 1930s, Adolf Hitler decreed that superior people were tall, strong, blond, blue-eyed, heterosexual Christian people of Germanic background, whom he called Aryans. His plan was to create a so-called master race, which would consist solely of Aryans, and he set about this plan by brutally eliminating those who did not fit his blueprint—mainly Jews, but also Gypsies, homosexuals, Catholics, and others he deemed undesirable. He had them rounded up by the thousands and

Driven by the dream of establishing a master race, Adolf Hitler ruthlessly massacred Jews, Gypsies, homosexuals, the mentally ill, and anyone else who differed from his Aryan ideal.

sent to concentration camps. More than 6 million people were killed—the overwhelming majority of them Jews. Hitler offers the most terrible example of what can happen when someone decides to "improve" the human race. One type of person is valued highly; the rest are valued not at all.

This notion of improving the human race by selecting certain genetic types or by manipulating genes is called eugenics. Some thinkers are concerned that cloning could be used as a eugenic tool.

The fear is not so much that a "master race" would actually be created. After all, it would be very hard for even the most powerful dictator to use cloning as a practical eugenic method. Such a dictator would have to persuade thousands of women to allow cloned embryos to be implanted in their wombs, to carry them, and to give birth to them—an unlikely scenario. The more realistic concern is that human cloning might indirectly end up working as a form of eugenics.

How cloning might affect society

Cloning is never going to be the most popular method of having children. No matter how technically easy it becomes, most people will probably choose to have their babies in the usual way. But if cloning *did* become available, some people would surely take advantage of it. Who might those people be?

Probably the main deciding factor would be money. Considering that cloning would be an expensive process, whoever these people might be, they would probably be wealthy. Richard Seed, who intends to start human cloning clinics, says his clones will cost "under $1 million." Unless his price was very much under that amount, not many people would be able to afford it. The option of having a child by cloning would be limited to wealthy people, and in this country wealthy people are likely to be white. So cloning would become, in a sense, a eugenic tool: it would function as a way of producing more rich white people.

Writer David Shenk has thought about this possibility. He is troubled by the idea that the benefits of genetic con-

Borgman/*Cincinnati Enquirer.* Reprinted by special permission of King Features Syndicate.

trol would belong only to the wealthy classes. People who could afford cloning would be able to pass on not only their wealth but their genes to their children, giving them still another advantage over those with less money. The rich could *choose* to have children who were tall, slender, strong, and apt to have a high IQ. The poor would have to take their chances, as people have always done before. If this were to go on for many generations, Shenk foresees a time when the differences between rich and poor "could become so great that humans will be literally transformed into more than one species."[31]

Not everyone shares Shenk's concern. For that kind of transformation to take place, huge numbers of people would have to be cloned. Lee Silver, of Princeton University, does not think that this is going to happen. "Even if this technology becomes safe and efficient," he says, "we're talking about a small number of people that will want to use it. It's not going to have any effect on society at large."[32]

Still, human cloning would have an effect on the individuals who use it, even if there are only a few of them, and this raises a question that underlies the entire moral debate: Is it right for *any* people, rich or poor, to have so much control over an area of human life that was previously governed by nature? The only way to answer this question is to consider what kinds of harm might result.

The risk of physical harm

Scientists cannot be sure, at this point, that cloning a human being would be safe. There is a risk of miscarriage as well as a risk that a child originated by cloning would be abnormal in some unpredictable way. Most participants in the cloning debate agree that research to prove that cloning is safe should be done before cloning a human being is even considered. But how safe is safe enough?

Even the ordinary method of human reproduction is not completely safe. Pregnant women miscarry; births can go wrong; children can be born with defects. Some experts say that it makes no sense to insist that cloning be proved perfectly safe before it can be done. A certain amount of risk is involved in most of what people do, they say; cloning should be no different. "People exaggerate the fears of the unknown and downplay the very real dangers of the familiar," says Gregory Pence. "In a very important sense, driving a car each day is far more dangerous to children than the new form of human reproduction under discussion here. Many, many people are hurt and killed every day in automobile wrecks, yet few people consider not driving."[33]

Some standard of safety will have to be established before human cloning can be done, but it may be difficult for people to reach an agreement on what that standard should be.

High expectations

Suppose a couple decided to have a child by cloning a favorite uncle. As that child grows up, the parents might well expect him to be like his uncle—just as smart, just as athletic, just as good at the clarinet. The child might feel these expectations as pressure. He might feel that he does not have the freedom to be what *he* wants to be.

Many critics of human cloning are afraid that this would happen. "Cloning parents will have expectations," says Leon Kass. "The child is given a genotype that has already lived, with full expectations that this blueprint of a past life ought to be controlling of the life that is to come. Cloning

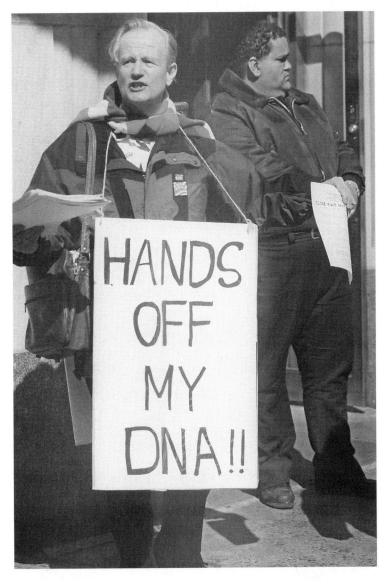

Many people voice ethical objections to cloning, particularly the potential misuse of DNA and the technology's possible emotional side effects.

is inherently despotic, for it seeks to make one's children (or someone else's children) after one's own image (or an image of one's choosing) and their future according to one's will."[34]

Of course, parents have expectations for their children now. They expect their children to be like them, at least to a certain extent. They expect their children to do well in school and to be socially successful. It is possible, however, that the expectations for a clone would be more intense than for an ordinary child.

Production versus procreation

To have children is to take a chance. Parents cannot know what their child will be like; they commit themselves to loving and caring for whatever child they happen to have. Technology, however, is already giving parents new kinds of choices about having children. Those who would rather have a girl than a boy, or vice versa, can be assisted by techniques that favor the development of the preferred sex. Single women can choose to use sperm from a sperm bank to conceive a child. They can look through catalogs that describe the sperm donors and choose the one whose qualities they like best. There is even a sperm bank that stores the frozen sperm of men of great talent and high achievement, which might be the choice of a parent who hopes for an exceptionally smart and talented child.

But cloning would bring the notion of "designer children" closer to reality. Maybe those who could afford to would have their children "made to order"—cloned from adults who are thought to have turned out well. To some, this is an offensive idea; it seems more like purchasing a product than having a child.

Gilbert Meilaender, a Lutheran theologian who writes about bioethics, is one who holds this view. Having a baby by means of cloning, he says, would be "far less a surrender to the mystery of the genetic lottery . . . [and] far more an understanding of the child as a product of human will."[35]

He believes that if people start trying to make children according to their own ideas, instead of submitting to the will of God and accepting whatever child comes to them, something sacred will be lost.

Leon Kass, too, thinks that cloning would be the wrong way to make a child: "Human cloning," he says, "would represent a giant step toward turning begetting into making, procreation into manufacture."[36] What's wrong with "manufacturing" a child? Kass and others who share his point of view see several harmful consequences. One of them is a change in the relationship between parents and children. Instead of being "a gift from heaven," as children are often thought of now, the child would be more like something its parents had *crafted,* as they might craft a doll or a puppet, for example, choosing what it should look like and what its abilities should be. The parents might feel a new and unwholesome kind of power, as if they had *made* their child rather than received it. "As with any product of our making, no matter how excellent," Kass says, "the artificer stands above it, not as an equal but as a superior, transcending it by his will and creative prowess. . . . In human cloning, scientists and prospective 'parents' would be adopting the same technocratic mentality to human children: human children would be their artifacts. Such an arrangement is profoundly dehumanizing, no matter how good the product."[37]

Defending cloning

Not everyone, however, thinks it would be dehumanizing to deliberately choose one's children's genes. The late bioethicist Joseph Fletcher took a position exactly opposite to that of Leon Kass. He did not think that using technology to reproduce human beings would be dehumanizing at all. In fact, he said, "laboratory reproduction is radically human compared to conception by ordinary heterosexual intercourse. It is willed, chosen, purposed and controlled, and surely those are among the traits that distinguish Homo sapiens from others in the animal genus, from the primates on down."[38]

In Seoul, protesters condemn scientists at a South Korean university for researching techniques to clone human cells and thereby create replacement organs.

Gregory Pence, who has written extensively in defense of human cloning, agrees: he sees nothing wrong with choosing to give a child the best possible genetic heritage. "Most of us," he writes, "would be happy if our parents had created us by attempting to give us a genetic inheritance free of cancer, heart disease, and progressive neurological disease by originating us from some person known to have lived into her nineties with an exuberance for life. If we applied the Golden Rule, it is reasonable to assume that—far from being depressed at such origination—most people would be glad to have been originated from the genotype of someone we now admire."[39]

Loss of human dignity

The phrase *human dignity* comes up often in the debate about cloning. Many opponents of cloning think that a clone would be deprived of the sense of personhood that is the right of every individual. One writer expresses it this way: "For there is already in the world another person, one's earlier twin, who from the same genetic starting point has made life choices that are still in the later twin's future. It will seem that one's life has already been lived

Catrow. Reprinted by permission of Copley News Service.

and played out by another, that one's fate is already determined, and so that later twin will lose the spontaneity of authentically creating and becoming his or her own self. One will lose the sense of human possibility in freely creating one's own future."[40]

Not only might the clone feel an insult to his or her human dignity, according to these thinkers, but other people might also view a clone the same way. Clones might be treated as less than human—they might suffer abuse and discrimination, as if they were an inferior class of people.

This would certainly be a problem, if it occurred. But not everyone thinks it would. "Why suppose that cloned persons wouldn't share the same rights and dignity as the rest of us?" says bioethicist Ruth Macklin. A cloned person, after all, would be indistinguishable from a person born any other way, and entitled to the same respect and the same protection of the law. If affronts to the human dignity of a clone occurred, Macklin feels, people's attitudes would be at fault, not the process of cloning. "A world not safe for cloned humans would be a world not safe for the rest of us,"[41] she says.

A child made for a purpose

The Ayalas, whose daughter was dying of leukemia, brought a new child into the world for a specific purpose: to save her sister's life. There are two opinions about this. One is that the Ayalas did the right thing. The other is that they did not: human beings, according to this view, should be created only for their own sake, never for someone else's purpose. A child should be an end in itself, not a means to another end. The hope for a daughter who could win beauty contests; the hope for a son who could be a baseball star; the hope for a baby to replace one who died—all these hopes have to do with the parents' purposes and not those of the child to be born. The result, in the opinion of some thinkers, is a disrespect for the child, who exists to fulfill its parents' desires rather than for its own sake.

Others, however, do not see that this problem has anything in particular to do with cloning. R. C. Lewontin, a professor of biology at Harvard University, points out that children are brought into the world to fulfill their parents' desires all the time. He does not see "how cloning would significantly increase the already immense number of children whose conception and upbringing were intended to make them instruments of their parents' frustrated ambitions, psychic fantasies, desires for immortality, or property calculations."[42]

Children are often conceived simply to fulfill a parent's desire to be a mother or a father. Does having such a purpose harm the child? Lewontin would argue that it does not. So would Lee Silver, who says, "If a child is born healthy and happy and it's loved by its parents, I don't think it matters how that child began its development."[43]

But even if it could be proved that creating a child by cloning was not harmful to either parents or children, the controversy about cloning would still not be resolved. There are many people, most of them guided by their religious beliefs, who *do* think it matters how a child begins its development. They hold that human beings should not tamper with the process of reproduction. The power to create human beings, they say, should belong only to God.

Trespassing on God's territory?

Shortly after the cloning of Dolly the sheep was announced, the Vatican, speaking for Pope John Paul II, issued a statement called "Reflections on Cloning." In it the pope condemns human cloning for many reasons, including damage to family relationships, the use of the human body as a research tool, and the injury to the human dignity of a clone, who might feel that he did not have his own identity. But the main point in the pope's message has to do with harm of a greater magnitude: "Cloning risks being the tragic parody of God's omnipotence."[44]

A parody is an imitation done so badly as to be ridiculous. People who attempt to clone human beings, the pope is saying, would be trying to imitate the creative power of God, and doing a bad job of it. They would be interfering in an area where they had no business being. This would be tragic. It would be, from the religious viewpoint, a serious sin: the sin of pride, the sin of believing that a human being can have as much power as God.

In March 1997, shortly after the cloning of Dolly was announced, *Time* magazine ran a poll, asking people this question: "Is it against God's will to clone human beings?"[45] Seventy-four percent of the people who responded

Pope John Paul II has denounced human cloning as being inconsistent with the tenets of Catholicism and a trespass on God's authority.

answered yes. Probably most of these people knew very little, if anything, about cloning, except that it was a way of making a copy of a living thing. If they had been asked why they thought it was against God's will, they might not have been able to explain. But this feeling—that there is something unnatural, even unholy, about cloning—is deep and widespread in the American public.

At about the same time that the pope issued his "Reflections," the National Bioethics Advisory Commission, convened by President Clinton in 1997 to make recommendations about human cloning, released its report. In order to compose this report, the members of the commission had listened to a great deal of testimony from experts and ordinary citizens on all sides of the cloning issue. One of the comments they heard most often was that human cloning would be "playing God." Their report acknowledges this point of view. "Opponents assert that this new type of cloning tempts human beings to transgress moral boundaries and to grasp for powers that are properly outside human control," the report says. "In particular, humans should not consider themselves as omnipotent over nature."[46]

Drawing the line

This question of natural boundaries is central to the debate about human cloning. Many people believe there is a limit to what human beings should know and do; beyond that limit, the power belongs to God. But even those who say there should be some limit have trouble determining exactly where the limit is. What is the meaning of a natural boundary? One might say that to transplant a heart from one body to another crosses a natural boundary, and that doctors who perform such operations take on too much power over human life. Some people would probably say that surgery to reduce the size of a nose tampers with God's work. Certain religious sects believe that any medical treatment at all is counter to God's will. If the morality of cloning is to be decided on the basis of whether it is against God's will, people will first have to agree on what God's will is.

Pontius' Puddle. Reprinted by permission of Joel Kauffmann.

There seems to be general agreement among those with a religious viewpoint, however, that human reproduction is God's work alone. "There is strong and real understanding," says Rabbi Marc Gellman of Temple Beth Torah in New York, "that we are not our own creators. And this [cloning] technology undermines that fundamental belief in the most powerful and disturbing way possible."[47]

Part of God's plan?

As with every aspect of the human cloning question, there are those who disagree. Sociologist James Hughes, for example, does not think that cloning represents "a boundary beyond which humanity dare not go." He does not believe, he says, "that there is such a boundary. Humanity should be in control of its own destiny."[48]

Richard Seed, the scientist who wants to set up human cloning clinics, thinks that far from being against God's will, human cloning is part of God's long-range plan for the human race. Seed said in a radio interview, "God made man in his own image. God intended for man to become one with God. Cloning and the reprogramming of DNA is the first serious step in becoming one with God."[49]

Seed's is a fairly extreme point of view. Other thinkers, without presuming to decide which religious beliefs are right, simply caution against letting religion play too great a role in policy making about human cloning. "Surely everyone has the right to be heard," says the statement from the International Academy of Humanism. "But we believe the danger is very real that research with enormous

potential benefit may be suppressed solely because it con-
flicts with some people's religious beliefs. It is important
to recognize that similar religious objections were once
raised against autopsies, anesthesia, artificial insemination,
and the entire genetic revolution of our day—yet enormous
benefits have accrued from each of these developments."[50]

Reaching a compromise

There is no resolution in sight for the disagreement over
human cloning. Nevertheless, the research goes on, and the
technical possibility of a human clone becomes more real
every day. Some compromise has to be reached between
those who say human cloning must never happen, because
it is immoral, and those who say human cloning must happen, because its benefits far outweigh its dangers. As with
other issues on which people cannot agree, the legal system steps in.

6

Regulating
Human Cloning

ANY SCIENTIST WHO wanted to start a human
cloning project in the United States would have a par-
adoxical legal problem. Cloning a human being is not
against the law, but a great deal more research has to be
done before scientists will know how to clone a person
and whether doing so is safe. That research, however, *is*
against the law. So American scientists who want to inves-
tigate the possibilities of human cloning are stopped before they begin.

Lawmakers all over the world are struggling with the
questions that human cloning raises. Because the technology is so new, and because opinions about it are so deeply
divided, developing laws to govern it is very difficult. One
professor of bioethics, Glenn McGee, says bluntly, "We
are in a regulatory nightmare."[51]

The current laws

As soon as the cloning of Dolly the sheep was announced, alarmed government leaders began talking about
what should be done if human cloning became possible.
President Clinton's first action was to ban federal funding for research on human cloning. He also asked that all
researchers—even those who do not use federal funding—
agree to a moratorium on cloning research: no research for
five years, until more about cloning can be learned from
animal studies. Then he put together a panel of experts on

human cloning (the National Bioethics Advisory Commission, or NBAC) and gave them ninety days to make their recommendations.

At the same time, many states were making their own cloning laws. California and Michigan, for instance, have banned human cloning. Several other states, including Illinois, Ohio, Wisconsin, and Connecticut, are considering such a ban.

Other countries also rushed to declare their positions. Germany, Denmark, Australia, Spain, and the United Kingdom have all forbidden human cloning. In December 1997, nineteen European nations, including Finland, France, Greece, and Portugal, signed a treaty declaring that human cloning was a misuse of science and stating their intention to pass laws against it.

All this activity happened within months of the cloning of Dolly, even though no human beings had as yet been cloned and there was no agreement on whether human

Sargent. © Austin American Statesman. Reprinted by permission of Universal Press Syndicate. All rights reserved.

cloning was good or bad. These national and state leaders assumed, however, that some day human cloning would become possible and that there should be some preexisting regulations.

What those regulations should be, however, remains a matter of disagreement. The NBAC summed up the balance that the laws would have to strike: "The challenge to public policy," said its report, "is to support the myriad beneficial applications of this new technology, while simultaneously guarding against its more questionable uses."[52] But it is hard to know how that should be done, especially when there is so much difference of opinion about which uses are beneficial and which are questionable.

The argument for a ban

Some people offer a simple answer to the legal question by saying that all human cloning, anywhere, for any purpose, should be banned. One of these is Leon Kass of the University of Chicago. "We should do all we can to prevent the cloning of human beings," he says. "We should do this by means of an international legal ban if possible, and by a unilateral national ban, at a minimum."[53]

Kass and those who share his viewpoint would like to make sure that no human clone is ever born, and the most efficient way to do this is to make a law that would apply to everyone in the country (or in the world, if possible). Such a law would make it a crime to clone a human being—a federal crime, punishable by a sizable fine and a prison term.

For the most part, the American people want the government to stay out of such private and personal areas as human reproduction, and in general the government does stay out. No laws tell parents whether they can have children, when they can have children, or how many. No federal regulations apply to clinics where *in vitro* fertilization is done. But thinkers like Kass consider cloning to be radically different from any other reproductive technology. They are afraid that scientists, hoping to be on the cutting edge of this new frontier, will move ahead too quickly with human cloning research. "Only government," says George Annas, professor of Health Law at Boston University, "has the authority to restrain science and technology until its social and moral implications are adequately examined."[54]

The argument against a ban

A complete, permanent ban on human cloning seems to other people, however, like a much-too-drastic measure. No one has proved yet that cloning a human being would necessarily cause harm. There is no reason to think, so far, that it would be any more dangerous than fertilizing an egg in a laboratory dish, which is done in fertility clinics across the nation. In any case, making cloning a federal crime seems extreme to critics of Kass's view. There are other kinds of misconduct that are not federal crimes. Sometimes, for example, surgeons perform operations without

Under extreme magnification, the four cells of a human embryo are clearly visible. Throughout the world, the possibility of cloning such embryos continues to be hotly debated.

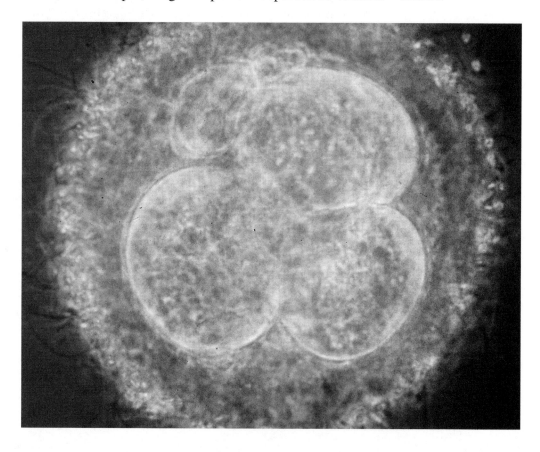

adequate preparation, which can be very dangerous—and yet there is no federal law against this. Why should cloning a human being be considered uniquely unlawful?

It would take a vote in Congress to pass a federal ban against human cloning. In ten or fifteen years, scientists working in other countries might prove that cloning poses no dangers, and that it is, in fact, of great value to medicine and to society. But it would take another act of Congress to change the law in the United States. This could be a difficult and time-consuming process.

The problem of research

The United States has not yet banned human cloning—but it has banned federal funding for research that might lead to human cloning, and this effectively stops such research, since 90 percent of scientific experimentation in this country is federally funded. The problem is that this same research could also lead to important discoveries that have nothing to do with making cloned babies. Scientists might use cloning technology to grow matching liver tissue for someone with liver disease or bone marrow for someone with leukemia; they might use it to learn more about how cells differentiate and why some cells become cancerous; they might use it to increase their understanding of human aging, and to eliminate some genetic diseases. But experiments like these would involve creating human embryos, and that is what makes this research so controversial.

Many people feel very strongly that researchers should never do experiments with human life. Those who hold this view are against not only the possibility of a human clone being born but also the fact that scientists would create human embryos in the laboratory, watch them develop up to a certain point, and then destroy them. "The production of human beings for the purpose of experiments that will destroy them should be prohibited by law," says a statement of the Ramsey Colloquium, a group of Jewish and Christian theologians and scholars. "The use of human beings for experiments that will do them harm and to

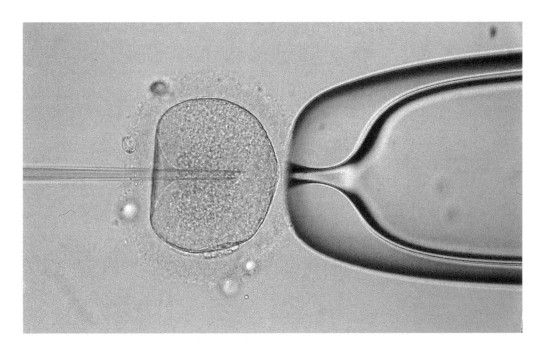

which they have not given their consent should be prohibited by law. It matters not how young or how small, how
old or how powerless, such human beings may be."[55]

An opinion such as this one is based on the conviction
that a human embryo, even one that consists of only a few
cells, is a human being, with all the rights to protection of
any person, because it has the potential to grow into a person. But there are some who argue against this. To say
that an embryo consisting of a few cells is a person,
points out Gregory Pence, "is like saying an acorn is a
twenty-year-old, 60-foot-tall oak tree in value and con-
cept. But if I pick up an acorn from your yard, you do not
charge me with theft, but you would if I cut down your
mature oak tree." Pence points out that other countries allow research on human embryos until they are fourteen
days old. He believes that the benefits of such research far
outweigh any harm done. "It makes sense," he says, "to
think that an eight-month-old fetus is almost a person but
an eight-cell embryo is not. The challenge is now to find a
way to fund research on human embryos to help those of
us who are persons."[56]

During the process of in vitro fertilization, a lab technician uses a flat-nosed pipette (right) to brace a human egg that is being injected with DNA.

Federal funds for experiments

There are two ways of looking at the ban on federal funds for human cloning research. One view says that banning funds is right because it discourages such research. The other view says that banning funds might actually cause the harm it is meant to prevent. When the government provides money for research, it also has some control over that research. But the government has no role in research that goes on in private labs. Experiments there would not take place in the public eye; if they were dangerous or unethical, no one would know. So nearly all of the participants in the human cloning debate agree that some research should be funded, and that government regulations for it should be put in place.

The NBAC drew a clear line in its recommendation: some research on human embryos should be allowed, it said, but making a child by means of cloning should be a federal crime. No cloned embryo should be implanted in a woman's womb, there to grow into a baby. The commission added, however, that a "sunset clause" should be included in whatever law is drawn up. A sunset clause specifies a time in the future when the law can be reexamined in the light of research that has been done since the law was made. If, in ten years or so, research has reassured those who object to human cloning, then any laws against it that might be made now could be reconsidered.

What experiments are acceptable?

Opponents of human cloning acknowledge that research using cloning technology could lead to medical benefits. So some of them have proposed that such research should be allowed and funded by the government, but *only* if the researchers can prove that what they intend to do has a valuable social purpose. This means that someone at a government agency, probably the National Institutes of Health, would have to decide whether a proposed experiment is a valuable one or not. George Annas, professor of Health Law at Boston University, thinks a human experimentation agency should be established in order to review cloning proposals and approve or disapprove them, according to whether they are good for society.

But ideas of what is good for society vary greatly from one person to another. Say the purpose of the experiment were to give an infertile couple the chance to have a biologically related child, for example. Is that an important enough purpose? It is important to the couple who wants the child, but they might feel it was unjust to have to prove that their desire for a child was important to society. "When have Americans ever been subjected to such a requirement before they were allowed to have children?"[57] asks Gregory Pence.

Those on Pence's side of the issue believe that the burden of proof should be on the opponents of cloning and cloning research. They believe strongly that in matters that have to do with the family, freedom of choice must be protected. Those who want to limit that freedom should have to give good reasons for doing so. They should have to prove that cloning would be harmful in some way before preventing people from doing it.

Will the laws be enforceable?

Sooner or later, governments of states and countries will decide on laws to regulate human cloning. It is likely that many countries will follow the lead of nations such as Germany and Spain and ban human cloning altogether. Even if every country in the world made cloning illegal, however, it is not certain that those laws could be enforced. When an exciting new technology is discovered, the urge to develop it and use it is very strong. "This technology is not, in principle, policeable,"[58] says Dr. Ronald Munson of the University of Missouri.

He is probably right, for several reasons. One reason is that the technology is advancing so quickly that a law made today might not be useful tomorrow. In California, for example, human cloning is against the law—that is, it is illegal to replace the nucleus of a human egg with genetic material from another human cell, the technique

Wilmut used to clone Dolly. But researchers at the University of Wisconsin are working on a method that would enable human cells to be put into cow eggs. If this method were used in California, it could result in the cloning of a human embryo and still not technically be against the law.

It is hard to predict all the legal questions that human cloning would raise—and therefore, hard to make laws about them ahead of time. Lawyers may have to decide, for example, whether it should be legal for a person to sell his or her own genome (collection of the genes of an organism). A person of great fame or extraordinary skills might want to charge thousands of dollars for a few skin cells, if someone wanted to make a clone of him or her, or might charge many times that much if many clones were made. Laws will have to be developed if these events transpire.

If cloning became an acceptable way to have a child, situations such as this might come about: A couple has a child by creating a clone of the husband. Some years later, the couple divorces. They argue over the custody of the child. The husband might claim that he is the child's only true parent because the child shares his genes and does not share the mother's. A judge might have a hard time deciding how to rule.

The strongest drive behind human cloning, the thing that will make law enforcement most difficult, will probably be the marketplace. Lee Silver, of Princeton University, has doubts about the ability of laws to prevent human cloning. "Cloning might proceed," he says, "even if the government is against it, even if scientists are against it, even if ethicists are against it, if there are people willing to pay money."[59] Already one person, Richard Seed, has announced that he will go ahead with his cloning project even if it means moving to another country in order to escape the legal prohibition. As long as

Harold Varmus (center), the director of the National Institutes of Health, and Ian Wilmut (left) testify during the March 12, 1997, Senate subcommittee hearings on cloning.

there are people who, for whatever reason, want to be cloned and have enough money to spend on the process, there are likely to be doctors or other scientists who will be willing to offer the service.

"They'll never be forgotten"

Fame is another motivation. Ian Wilmut is famous around the world for making the first clone of an adult mammal. That much fame and more would come to the scientist who made the first human clone. "You can make cloning against the law but I think people will try anyway," says Jon Gordon, of Mount Sinai Hospital in New York. "They'll do it because if they do, they'll never be forgotten."[60]

Of course, just because people are going to bypass the law does not mean that a law should not be made. Laws about cloning will continue to be made. Some people will probably break them or find ways to get around them, and the laws will be rewritten as new situations arise. In the long run, this is part of the process necessary for working out ways to deal with a technology that is so new and has such tremendous potential as human cloning.

Notes

Introduction

1. Quoted in Gina Kolata, *Clone: The Road to Dolly, and the Path Ahead.* New York: William Morrow, 1998, p. 89.

***Chapter 1: Flowers, Farms, and Forests:
Cloning in Agriculture***

2. Quoted at Linda's Orchid Page, www.orchidlady.com.

3. Quoted in Tim Friend, "Firms Work on Building a Better Tree," *USA Today,* The Nation's Homepage, July 1, 1998. http://archives.usatoday.com/.

4. Michael D. Bishop, ABS Global, Inc., press release from *Infigen,* August 7, 1997. www.infigen.com/newsrel-frame.htm.

5. Donald Bruce, "Should We Clone Animals?" Society, Religion and Technology Project of the Church of Scotland, 1996. http://webzone1.co.uk/www/srtproject/clonan1.htm.

6. Bruce, "Should We Clone Animals?"

Chapter 2: Cloning in Medicine

7. Quoted in Andrew Ross, "Dr. Frankenstein, I Presume?" *Salon,* February 1997. www.salonmagazine.com/feb97/news/news2970224.html.

8. Quoted in Kenneth Chang, "Dolly's Sequels Make Drugs," 1998, ABCNEWS.com.

9. Quoted in Ross, "Dr. Frankenstein, I Presume?"

10. Quoted in Piotr Skawinski, "Animal Organ Transplants Create Doubts as Well as Cures." http://ssmu.mcgill.ca/trib/current/organ.html.

11. Quoted in Skawinski, "Animal Organ Transplants."

12. Quoted in Australian Broadcasting Corporation, "Transplanting Animal Organs into Humans," an interview for Radio National, August 12, 1996. www.abc.net.au/rn/talks/8.30/helthrpt/hstories/hr120896.htm.

13. Alan H. Berger, "Animals as Spare Parts," presentation at Conference: The Ethics of Genetic Engineering and Animal Patents, University of Wisconsin, Madison, October 12, 1996. www.api4animals.org/xenola.htm.

14. Statement of the Foundation for Biomedical Research. www.fbresearch.org/quests.htm.

15. People for the Ethical Treatment of Animals, information page on cloning. www.peta-online.org.

16. Quoted in Ross, "Dr. Frankenstein, I Presume?"

Chapter 3: Cloning Endangered Species

17. Quoted in Amanda Onion, "Scientists Debate Merits and Methods of Cloning the Endangered Giant Panda," Fox News Online, July 28, 1998. www.foxnews.com/scitech/072898/panda.sml.

18. Quoted in Philip Cohen, "Cloning Special Report: Crunch Time: Could Cloning Rescue Pandas from Extinction?" *New Scientist,* January 24, 1998. www.nsplus.com/nsplus/insight/clone/crunch.html.

19. Quoted in George Poinar and Roberta Poinar, *The Quest for Life in Amber.* New York: Addison-Wesley, 1994, pp. 93–94.

20. Quoted in Jan Hollingsworth, "Extinction Crisis," *Tampa Tribune,* April 21, 1998. www.tampatrib.com/news/enviro23.htm.

Chapter 4: Cloning Human Beings

21. Quoted in Kolata, *Clone,* p. 4.

22. Arthur Caplan, "Bah Cloning," *Philadelphia Inquirer,* March 4, 1997.

23. Reuters News Service, "Richard Seed Offers to Clone Human Race," *New Zealand Herald,* January 9, 1998. http://matu1.math.auckland.ac.nz/~king/Preprints/book/genes/genaug/seedc.htm.

24. "Opposition to Human Cloning Will 'Blow Over,' Scientist Says," CNN, January 7, 1998. http://netra.wow.net.tw/~uforael/clone2.htm.

25. Quoted in Gregory E. Pence, ed., *Flesh of My Flesh: The Ethics of Cloning Humans: A Reader.* New York: Rowman & Littlefield, 1998, p. 10.

26. Quoted in Kolata, *Clone,* p. 231.

Chapter 5: Questions of Right and Wrong

27. Quoted in Jeffrey Kluger, "Will We Follow the Sheep?" *Time,* March 10, 1997.

28. Gregory E. Pence, *Who's Afraid of Human Cloning?* New York: Rowman & Littlefield, 1998, p. 63.

29. Leon Kass, "The Wisdom of Repugnance," in Pence, *Flesh of My Flesh,* p. 18.

30. International Academy of Humanism, "International Academy of Humanism Issues Statement Supporting Cloning Research," press release, May 16, 1997. www.secularhumanism.org/pr/cloning_05_97.text.

31. David Shenk, "Biocapitalism: What Price the Genetic Revolution?" *Harper's,* December 1997.

32. Quoted in "Multiplying Issues," PBS NewsHour transcript, January 8, 1998. www.pbs.org/newshour/bb/science/jan-june98/cloning.

33. Pence, *Flesh of My Flesh,* p. 119.

34. Quoted in Pence, *Flesh of My Flesh,* p. 31.

35. Quoted in Pence, *Who's Afraid?* p. 27.

36. Leon Kass, "For an International Ban." Testimony presented to the National Bioethics Advisory Commission,

March 14, 1997, Washington, DC. www.texasrighttolife.com/cloning/abacreport_04.html.

37. Kass, "For an International Ban."

38. Quoted in Pence, *Who's Afraid?* p. 125.

39. Pence, *Who's Afraid?* p. 136.

40. Quoted in Pence, *Flesh of My Flesh,* p. 51.

41. Ruth Macklin, "Human Cloning? Don't Just Say No," *U.S. News & World Report,* March 10, 1997.

42. Quoted in Pence, *Flesh of My Flesh,* p. 135.

43. Quoted in "Multiplying Issues," PBS NewsHour transcript.

44. Juan de Dios Vial Correa and Elio Sgreccia, "Reflections on Cloning," Pontificia Academia Pro Vita, Libreria Editrice Vaticana, 1997. www.vatican.va/roman_curia/pontifical_academies/acdlife/documents/rc_pont-acd_life_doc_30091997_clon_en.shtml.

45. Quoted in Kluger, "Will We Follow the Sheep?" p. 71.

46. Quoted in Pence, *Flesh of My Flesh,* p. 55.

47. Quoted in Pence, *Who's Afraid?* p. 124.

48. Quoted in Pence, *Who's Afraid?* p. 124.

49. "Opposition to Human Cloning Will 'Blow Over,' Scientist Says," CNN.

50. International Academy of Humanism, press release.

Chapter 6: Regulating Human Cloning

51. Quoted in Rick Weiss, "Firm Says It Created Embryo Out of Human, Cow Cells," *Washington Post,* November 13, 1998, p. A01. www.washingtonpost.com/wp-srv/national/science/cloning/keystories.

52. Quoted in Pence, *Flesh of My Flesh,* p. 59.

53. Quoted in Pence, *Flesh of My Flesh,* p. 34.

54. Quoted in Pence, *Flesh of My Flesh,* p. 82.

55. Ramsey Colloquium, "The Inhuman Use of Human Beings: A Statement on Embryo Research," *First Things,* no. 49, January 1995. www.firstthings.com/ftissues/ft9501/ramsey.html.

56. Pence, *Who's Afraid?* p. 88.

57. Pence, *Who's Afraid?* p. 154.

58. Quoted in Ross, "Dr. Frankenstein, I Presume?"

59. Quoted in "Multiplying Issues," PBS NewsHour transcript.

60. Quoted in Philip Cohen, "Cloning Special Report: Crossing the Line," *New Scientist,* January 17, 1998. www.nsplus.com/nsplus/insight/clone/crossing.html.

Glossary

bioethics: The study of questions of right and wrong that arise from the new biotechnologies.

chromosomes: Threadlike structures—in the nucleus of cells—that carry genetic information.

clone: A genetic duplicate of a living thing.

cystic fibrosis: A genetic disease that causes thick mucus to form and makes breathing difficult.

despotic: Tyrannical; ruling with absolute authority.

differentiation: In cells, the process of changing from the kind of cell that can develop into any part of the body to a cell of one specific kind.

DNA: Deoxyribonucleic acid, which is the name of the chemical from which a cell's genetic material is made.

embryo: The earliest stage in the development of a person or animal.

eugenics: The idea of improving the human race through the control or manipulation of genes.

genes: Sets of instructions made up of DNA. They tell the cell what to do and determine the characteristics of living things.

genome: A complete set of genes; all of one person's genes, taken together, are that person's genome.

hemophilia: A genetic disease that prevents blood from clotting properly.

in vitro **fertilization:** A technique in which a woman's egg is fertilized with a man's sperm in a laboratory dish rather than inside the woman's body (*in vitro* translated literally means "in glass").

moratorium: A delay or stopping of a certain activity.

nucleus: The part of a cell that contains the genetic material.

procreation: The creating of offspring by a male and a female.

tissue culture: The technique of generating plants by using cells from one plant to grow another that is genetically identical.

twinning: Causing an embryo to split in half, producing two identical embryos.

xenotransplant: The transplant of an organ from one species into another species—from a pig into a human being, for example.

Organizations
to Contact

Roslin Institute
Roslin, Midlothian, EH25 9PS UK
44-131-527-4200
fax: 44-131-440-0434
Internet: www2.ri.bbsrc.ac.uk/library/intro.html

The Roslin Institute in Scotland is where the cloning of Dolly the sheep took place. Information is available about the institute's activities. The institute also has a website that includes a special section on cloning.

San Diego Zoo
P.O. Box 120551
San Diego, CA 92112-0551
(619) 234-3153
Internet: www.sandiegozoo.org

The San Diego Zoo directs the Center for the Reproduction of Endangered Species. Information and updates on the attempt to save endangered giant pandas are available at their website.

University of Pennsylvania Center for Bioethics
3401 Market St., #320
Philadelphia, PA 19104-3308
(215) 898-7136
fax: (215) 573-3036

Internet: www.med.upenn.edu/bioethic/cgi/none.cgi

A well-known forum for discussion of bioethics issues, directed by Arthur Caplan.

Suggestions for Further Reading

Books

David Darling, *Beyond 2000: Genetic Engineering, Redrawing the Blueprint of Life.* Parsippany, NJ: Dillon Press, 1995. A simple introduction to the field of genetics, covering both scientific aspects and ethical issues.

Margery Facklam and Howard Facklam, *From Cell to Clone.* New York: Harcourt Brace Jovanovich, 1979. Not a new book, but one that provides useful background on genetics, as well as sections on the cloning of plants and possible future uses of animal cloning.

Dorothy Hinshaw Patent, *Biodiversity.* New York: Clarion Books, 1996. A beautifully illustrated book about the importance of appreciating and preserving the planet's biodiversity.

Rebecca Stefoff, *Extinction.* New York: Chelsea House, 1992. The author describes the causes of the mass extinctions occurring in recent years and suggests ways in which biodiversity can be preserved. Illustrated with photographs.

Periodicals

C. Freiman-Stiefel, "Cloning: Good Science or Baaaaad Idea?" *Science World,* May 2, 1997.

D. Hogan, "A Troubling Prospect," *Current Science,* May 16, 1997.

Junior Scholastic, "Should Human Cloning Be Allowed?" February 9, 1998.

S. J. O'Meara, "Dolly! Is That Really 'Ewe'?" *Odyssey,* May 1997.

A. Ragan, "Cloning: Are Humans Next?" *Junior Scholastic,* April 11, 1997.

Scope, "Should the Cloning of Human Beings Be Illegal?" April 18, 1997.

Websites

National Bioethics Advisory Commission (http://bioethics. gov/cgi-bin/AT-bioethicssearch.cgi). This is the commission convened by President Clinton to consider the issues of human cloning. Transcripts of their debates are available at their website, along with recent news about cloning and other bioethical issues.

New Scientist Planet Science (www.nsplus.com/nsplus/ insight/clone/clone.html). This website, which includes a picture of Dolly, contains many readable articles about cloning and issues related to cloning. A great variety of subjects is covered here. New Scientist Planet Science is the website of *New Scientist* magazine.

Science Explained (www.synapse.ndirect.co.uk/science/ clone.html). A clear, complete, and accessible explanation (with pictures and diagrams) of the process Ian Wilmut used to clone Dolly. Opportunity to send letters to website editor, Jamie Love. Recommendations for books and other related websites. Humorous tone.

Works Consulted

Books

Lee Gutkind, *Many Sleepless Nights.* New York: Norton, 1988. An in-depth exploration of the world of organ transplants.

Gina Kolata, *Clone: The Road to Dolly, and the Path Ahead.* New York: William Morrow, 1998. The definitive book about the cloning of Dolly the sheep, by the reporter who broke the story in the United States. Includes a description of earlier cloning attempts, explains Ian Wilmut's experiment in detail, and examines some of the issues that the new technology raises.

Charles C. Mann and Mark L. Plummer, *Noah's Choice: The Future of Endangered Species.* New York: Knopf, 1995. The authors deal with questions about the accelerating extinctions of America's wildlife species and the battle to balance human needs with preservation efforts.

Robert Massie and Suzanne Massie, *Journey.* New York: Knopf, 1975. One couple's account of the struggles involved in raising their hemophiliac son is a personal story that is full of information.

Sharon McAuliffe and Kathleen McAuliffe, *Life for Sale.* New York: Coward, McCann & Geoghegan, 1981. Fairly technical report on the state of genetic engineering as of 1981.

Gregory E. Pence, *Who's Afraid of Human Cloning?* New York: Rowman & Littlefield, 1998. Pence argues that fears about human cloning are unjustified; he deals with all the major issues.

Gregory E. Pence, ed., *Flesh of My Flesh: The Ethics of Cloning Humans: A Reader.* New York: Rowman & Littlefield, 1998. An anthology of essays by prominent thinkers on both sides of the human cloning controversy.

George Poinar and Roberta Poinar, *The Quest for Life in Amber.* New York: Addison-Wesley, 1994. Explains what the authors have learned from studying insects trapped in amber eons ago, and includes speculation about using ancient DNA to reproduce ancient creatures.

Doris M. Stone, *The Lives of Plants, Exploring the Wonders of Botany.* New York: Charles Scribner's Sons, 1983. A botanist's explanation of the structure and function of plants, including a chapter on cloning.

Colin Tudge, *The Engineer in the Garden.* New York: Hill and Wang, 1993. A respected science writer tells the story of genetics—its history and its possible future directions.

Edward O. Wilson, *The Diversity of Life.* Cambridge, MA: The Belknap Press of Harvard University Press, 1992. A major work by an internationally renowned expert, defining biodiversity and explaining its importance.

Cecil Woodham-Smith, *The Great Hunger.* London: Four Square Books, 1965. An account of the Irish Potato Famine.

Periodicals

Arthur Caplan, "Bah Cloning," *Philadelphia Inquirer,* March 4, 1997.

Sang-hun Choe, "Move Made Toward Human Cell Cloning," *Washington Post,* December 16, 1998.

Steven Connor, "British Scientists Seek Permission to Clone Human Building Blocks," *San Francisco Chronicle,* November 8, 1998.

Rod Fee, "Well . . . hello, Dolly!" *Successful Farming,* May/June 1997.

David Kestenbaum, "Cloning Plan Spawns Ethics Debate," *Science,* January 10, 1998.

Jeffrey Kluger, "Will We Follow the Sheep?" *Time,* March 10, 1997.

Michael Lemonick, "Dolly, You're History," *Time,* August 3, 1998.

Ruth Macklin, "Human Cloning? Don't Just Say No," *U.S. News & World Report,* March 10, 1997.

Oliver Morton, "First Dolly, Now Headless Tadpoles," *Science,* October 31, 1997.

Jeremy Rifkin, "The Second Genesis," *Maclean's,* May 4, 1998.

San Francisco Chronicle, "South Korean Scientists Say They Cloned Human Embryo," December 17, 1998, p. A10.

David Shenk, "Biocapitalism: What Price the Genetic Revolution?" *Harper's,* December 1997.

Allen Verhey, "Theology After Dolly: Cloning and the Human Family," *Christian Century,* March 19, 1997.

Christopher Wills, "A Sheep in Sheep's Clothing," *Discover,* January 1998.

Robert Wright, "Can Souls Be Xeroxed?" *Time,* March 10, 1997.

Internet Sources

Peter Aldhous, "The Fears of a Clone," *New Scientist,* February 21, 1998. www.nsplus.com/nsplus/insight/clone/fears.

Annual Report of the Roslin Institute, Edinburgh, 1996–97. www2.ri.bbsrc.ac.uk/library/annrep/annreps.html.

Australian Broadcasting Corporation, "Transplanting Animal Organs into Humans," an interview for Radio National, August 12, 1996. www.abc.net.au/rn/talks/8.30/helthrpt/hstories/hr120896.htm.

BBC News, "Human Spare-Part Cloning Set for Approval," December 8, 1998. http://news.bbc.co.uk/hi/english/sci/tech/newsid_230000/2300002.stm.

Alan H. Berger, "Animals as Spare Parts," presentation at Conference: The Ethics of Genetic Engineering and Animal Patents, University of Wisconsin, Madison, October 12, 1996. www.api4animals.org/xeno1a.htm.

Michael Bishop, ABS Global, Inc., press release from *Infigen*, August 7, 1997. www.infigen.com/newsrel-frame.htm.

Nell Boyce, "You Want to Clone? Go Ahead," *New Scientist,* May 9, 1998. www.nsplus.com/nsplus/insight/clone/goahead.

Donald Bruce, "Should We Clone Animals?" Society, Religion and Technology Project of the Church of Scotland, 1996. http://webzone1.co.uk/www/srtproject/clonan1.htm.

Linda Carroll, "Cow Eggs Used to Clone Other Animals—Human Cloning Could Now Develop Faster," MSNBC, undated. www.msnbc.com/news/13771.asp.

Kenneth Chang, "Dolly's Sequels Make Drugs," 1998. ABCNEWS.com.

Sang-hun Choe, "Move Made Toward Human Cell Cloning," *Washington Post,* December 16, 1998. http://wp6.washingtonpost.com/wp-srv/national/science/cloning/keystories/japan120998.htm.

"Cloning Seen Helping Save China's Panda," Fox News, March 17, 1997. www.foxnews.com/scitech/wires/t_0317_2.

Philip Cohen, "Cloning Special Report: Crossing the Line," *New Scientist,* January 17, 1998. www.nsplus.com/nsplus/insight/clone/crossing.html.

———, "Cloning Special Report: Crunch Time: Could Cloning Rescue Pandas from Extinction?" *New Scientist,* January 24, 1998. www.nsplus.com/nsplus/insight/clone/crunch.html.

Juan de Dios Vial Correa and Elio Sgreccia, "Reflections on Cloning," Pontificia Academia Pro Vita, Libreria Editrice Vaticana, 1997. www.vatican.va/roman_curia/pontifical_academies/acdlife/documents/rc_pont-acd_life_doc_30091997_clon_en.shtml.

Foundation for Biomedical Research. www.fbresearch.org/quests.htm.

Tim Friend, "Firms Work on Building a Better Tree," *USA Today,* The Nation's Homepage, July 1, 1998. http://archives.usatoday.com/.

Jan Hollingsworth, "Extinction Crisis," *Tampa Tribune,* April 21, 1998. www.tampatrib.com/news/enviro23.htm.

International Academy of Humanism, "International Academy of Humanism Issues Statement Supporting Cloning Research," press release, May 16, 1997. www.secularhumanism.org/pr/cloning_05_97.text.

Leon Kass, "For an International Ban." Testimony presented to the National Bioethics Advisory Commission, March 14, 1997, Washington, DC. www.texasrighttolife.com/cloning/abacreport_04.html.

Linda's Orchid Page. www.orchidlady.com.

Jamie Love, "The Cloning of Dolly," *Science Explained,* January 15, 1998. www.synapse.ndirect.co.uk/science/clone.html.

Usha Lee McFarling, "18 Months After Dolly, Cloning Is Becoming Commonplace," *IdahoNews.com,* September 20, 1998. www.idahonews.com/092098/discover/25946.htm.

"Multiplying Issues," PBS NewsHour transcript, January 8, 1998. www.pbs.org/newshour/bb/science/jan-june98/cloning.

National Center for Genome Resources, "Human Cloning: Should It Be Done? What Would It Mean?—FAQ's." www.ncgr.org/gpi/odyssey/dolly-cloning/cloning_humans.

Amanda Onion, "Scientists Debate Merits and Methods of Cloning the Endangered Giant Panda," Fox News Online, July 28, 1998. www.foxnews.com/scitech/072898/panda.sml.

"Opposition to Human Cloning Will 'Blow Over,' Scientist Says," CNN, January 7, 1998. http://netra.wow.net.tw/~uforael/clone2.htm.

People for the Ethical Treatment of Animals, information page on cloning. www.peta-online.org.

Ramsey Colloquium, "The Inhuman Use of Human Beings: A Statement on Embryo Research," *First Things,* no. 49, January 1995. www.firstthings.com/ftissues/ft9501/ramsey.html.

Philip R. Reilly and Dorothy C. Wertz, "The Future of Cloning," *The Gene Letter,* August 1998. www.geneletter.org/0898/twentyonearguments.htm.

Reuters News Service, "Richard Seed Offers to Clone Human Race," *New Zealand Herald,* January 9, 1998.

http://matu1.math.auckland.ac.nz/~king/Preprints/book/genes/genaug/seedc.htm.

Andrew Ross, "Dr. Frankenstein, I Presume?" *Salon,* February 1997. www.salonmagazine.com/feb97/news/news2970224.html.

Piotr Skawinski, "Animal Organ Transplants Create Doubts as Well as Cures." http://ssmu.mcgill.ca/trib/current/organ.html.

Bruno Sobral, "Genetic Tools for a Sustainable Future." www.ncgr.org/gpi/odyssey/green.

Texas Right to Life Committee, Inc., "Cloning: How the Pro-Life Issues Are Involved." www.texasrighttolife.com/cloning/abacreport_05.

Trade Environment Database, "Orchid Smuggling and Conservation," Case 199. http://gurukul.ucc.american.edu/TED/ORCHID.htm.

Charles Tritt, "The Ethics of Cloning of Humans from Somatic Cells." www.msoe.edu/~tritt/sf/cloning.humans.html.

U.S. House of Representatives, Committee on Science, Subcommittee on Technology, Washington, DC, "The Prohibition of Federal Government Funding of Human Cloning Research," July 22, 1997. www.commdocs.house.gov/committees/science/hsy203170.000/hsy203170_0.

Rick Weiss, "Cloned Calves Are 'Major Step' Toward Making Medicines in Milk," *Washington Post,* January 21, 1998. www.washingtonpost.com/wp-srv/national/science/cloning/keystories.

———, "Cow Eggs Play Crucial Role in Cloning Effort," *Washington Post,* January 19, 1998.

www.washingtonpost.com/wp-srv/national/science/
cloning/keystories.

——, "Fertility Experiments Mix Genes of Two Women," *Washington Post,* October 9, 1998. www.washingtonpost.
com/wp-srv/national/science/cloning/keystories.

——, "Firm Says It Created Embryo Out of Human, Cow Cells," *Washington Post,* November 13, 1998, p. A01.
www.washingtonpost.com/wp-srv/national/science/cloning/
keystories.

——, "Last Cow of Rare Breed Is Cloned in New Zealand," *Washington Post,* August 20, 1998. www.
washingtonpost.com/wp-srv/national/science/cloning/
keystories.

John Woolliams, "Nuclear Transfer: Uses of Cloning in Farm Animal Production," Annual Report 1996–97 of the Roslin Institute, Edinburgh, Scotland, pp. 24–25.
www2.ri.bbsrc.ac.uk/library/annrep/annreps.html.

Index

AIDS/HIV, 23, 27, 28
Alaska Frozen Tissue
  Collection, 43
alpha-1 antitrypsin, 24
animal clones
  Dolly, 6, 7–9, 47, 48
  Gene, 17
  Lady, 37–38
  planaria worm, 7
animal cloning, 6, 16–20
  arguments against, 19–20,
    29, 32–33
  disease-resistant herds and,
    18
  of endangered species,
    37–38, 39–40, 43
  extinct species and, 41–43
  failure rate in, 48
  vs. genetic diversity, 43–45
  of lambs, 49
  for medical research, 31–33
  of milk cows, 16–18
  for organ transplants,
    25–29
  twinning as, 17
Animal Protection Institute
  of America, 29
animal rights, 29
Annas, George, 79, 82–83
apple trees, 11–12
Aryans, 61–62

Audubon Center for
  Research on Endangered
  Species, 40
Australia, 77–78
Ayala, Abe and Mary,
  57–58, 70

baboons, 27
Baines, Michael, 28
Barnard, Christiaan, 25
Berger, Alan H., 29
biodiversity, 36–37
bioethics, 92
Blaiberg, Philip, 25
blood banks, 23
blood transfusions, 22–23
body repair kit, 30
bone marrow, 29–30, 57–58
brains, 54–55
Bruce, Donald, 19–20

California, 77–78, 83–84
Caplan, Arthur, 50
cells, 6, 43
  in animal cloning, 7–8, 23,
    40, 47
  in human cloning, 29–30,
    47, 83–84
  in plant cloning, 10–11, 15
Center for Bioethics
  (Pennsylvania), 50, 94–95

Center for Reproduction of
  Endangered Species, 43
chimpanzees, 27
chromosomes, 49–50, 92
Clinton, Bill, 73, 76–77
clones. *See* animal clones;
  human clones
cloning
  vs. evolutionary change, 45
  for medical purposes,
    23–25, 27, 30–31
  as research aid, 31–32,
    33–34
  see also animal cloning;
    human cloning; plant
    cloning
Connecticut, 77–78
cows, 17–18, 37–38, 48
  eggs of, 40–41, 51–52, 84
cymbidium orchids, 13–14
cystic fibrosis, 6, 24

dairy farmers, 16–18
Dawkins, Richard, 58
Defenders of Wildlife, 46
Denmark, 77–78
diabetes, 24
dinosaurs, 41–43
Dionne quintuplets, 54
diseases
  in animal-to-human
    transplants, 28
  cloned animals and, 18, 44
  of cloned plants, 12–13
  genetic disorders as, 6,
    21–24
  *see also names of specific
    diseases*

DNA, 40, 41, 42, 92
  mitochondrial, 53
Dolly (sheep), 6, 7–9, 47, 48
Dominko, Tanja, 41
Down's syndrome, 50
Dresser, Betsy, 40

embryos, 6, 38, 48
  chromosomes in, 49–50
  in cloning research, 80–81,
    82
  human, 47, 51, 62, 80–81,
    82
  implanted in related
    species, 38, 40–41, 51
  mitochondrial DNA and,
    53
  of pandas, 40
  sale of, 17–18
  twinning of, 17
endangered species, 36,
  37–40
  habitat preservation and,
    45–46
  tissue banks and, 43
eugenics, 62
extinction, species, 35–37
  DNA retrieval and, 41–43
  habitat preservation and, 46

Feinberg, Jay, 30
fertility clinics, 56, 78, 79
Finland, 77–78
Fletcher, Joseph, 67
Florida marshlands, 35
flowers, 10–11, 13–14
food crops, 11–13
ForBio (Australia), 14

forests, 14–15
Foundation for Biomedical
  Research, 33
France, 77–78

Gellman, Marc, 74
Gene (bull), 17
genes, 6, 56, 92
  in animal cloning, 7–8, 9,
    17, 23, 24, 32, 40–41
  defects in, 21, 24, 49–50,
    57
  eugenics and, 62
  genetic engineering and,
    18, 27
  of hemophiliacs, 21
  in plant cloning, 7, 12
genetic disorders, 21, 23
genetic diversity, 43–45
genetic engineering, 18
Germany, 77–78
Gordon, Jon, 85
Greece, 77–78
Griffin, Harry, 50

habitat preservation, 45–46
heart transplants, 25
hemophilia, 6, 21–23, 57
hepatitis, 23
Hitler, Adolf, 61–62
HIV/AIDS, 23, 27, 28
Hughes, James, 74
human clones
  brain development of,
    54–55
  could replace dead people,
    58, 70
  could save existing

children, 58, 70
  genetic parents of, 53
  might suffer discrimination,
    70
  will be "manufactured"
    children, 66–67
  will be subject to high
    expectations, 64–66
  will exist to fulfill parents'
    desires, 70–71
  will have limited sense of
    personhood, 69–70
human cloning, 47–49
  banning of, 76–80, 82
  basic steps of, 47, 52
  condemned by Pope John
    Paul II, 71–72
  defenders of, 67–69,
    74–75
  as eugenic tool, 62
  as federal crime, 78, 82
  federal funds for, 76, 80, 82
  for infertile couples, 56–57,
    83
  is morally unacceptable,
    60, 66–67, 73
  is not risky, 49–50
  is profound issue, 60,
    62–63, 65–67, 73–74
  is risky, 48–49, 64
  to make better people,
    61–62
  to prevent disease
    transmission, 57
  public opinion on, 72–73
  regulations on, 76–77, 80,
    82–86
  "sunset clause" for, 82

religious viewpoints on, 71–75
research on, 80, 82–84, 85
risk of miscarriages in, 48, 64
role of environment and, 53–56
safety standards for, 64, 76
to satisfy curiosity, 58
will be limited to wealthy people, 62–63, 66
women's eggs in, 51–52
see also human clones
Human Experimentation Agency, 82–83

Illinois, 77–78
immune systems, 26
infertile couples, 56–57, 78, 79, 83
Infigen (company), 17
International Academy of Humanism, 60, 74–75
in vitro fertilization, 56, 78
Irish Potato Famine, 12–13

James, Ron, 23
Johnson, George, 54
Jurassic Park (movie), 41–42

Kass, Leon, 60, 65, 67, 78

Lady (cow), 37–38
leukemia, 29–30, 57–58
Lewontin, R. C., 70–71
lumber industry, 14–15

Macklin, Ruth, 70

McCormick, Richard, 60
McGee, Glenn, 76
Meilaender, Gilbert, 66–67
Michigan, 77–78
miscarriages, 48, 49, 64
monkeys, 48
Munson, Ronald, 83
Murphy, Frederick, 28

National Bioethics Advisory Commission (NBAC), 73, 77, 78, 82
National Institutes of Health, 82
New York Times, 54
New Zealand cattle, 37–38

Ohio, 77–78
orange trees, 12
orchid plants, 13–14
organ transplants, 25–29, 54
cost of, 28–29

pandas, 38–40
Pence, Gregory, 60, 64, 68–69, 81, 83
People for the Ethical Treatment of Animals (PETA), 33
pigs, 27–28
planaria worm, 7
plant cloning, 7, 10–15
disease epidemics and, 12–13
of flowers, 10–11, 13–14
of food crops, 11–13
of forests, 14–15
pneumocystis, 26–27

Pope John Paul II, 71–72
Portugal, 77–78
potato crops, 11–13
PPL Laboratories (Scotland), 21, 23, 27
primates, 27

Ramsey Colloquium, 80–81
Raven, Peter, 36
reproductive technologies
  government regulation of, 78–79, 83
  in vitro fertilization as, 56, 78
  new choices in, 66
Roslin Institute (Scotland), 18, 24, 94
  site of Dolly's birth, 6

San Diego Zoo, 43, 94
Schlickeisen, Rodger, 46
Seed, Richard, 50, 62, 74, 85
sheep, 6, 7–9, 23, 24
Shenk, David, 62–63
Silver, Lee, 9, 63, 71, 85
skin grafting, 30
Spain, 77–78
sparrow, dusky seaside, 35, 37

species extinction. *See* extinction, species
sperm banks, 66

Teasdale, Bob, 15
Tector, Joseph, 28
Time magazine, 72–73
tissue banks, 30, 43
tissue culture, 10–11
Tkach, Jack, 41
transplant patients, 25–27
trees, 14–15
twinning, 17

United Kingdom, 77–78
U.S. Congress, 80

viruses, 28

Wilmut, Ian, 25, 34, 47, 85
  cloning experiments of, 7–8, 47, 48–49
  clotting factor and, 23
  human genetic disorders and, 21, 23
Wisconsin, 41, 77–78, 84
worm, planaria, 7

xenotransplant, 27–28

Picture Credits

Cover photo: Sipa Press
AP/Wide World Photos, 24, 44, 51, 57, 65, 68, 84
CC Studio/Science Photo Library/Photo Researchers,
    Inc., 81
Corbis, 12
Corbis/AFP, 38, 49
Corbis/Bettmann-UPI, 31
© Steve Kagan/Photo Researchers, Inc., 72
© Rafael Macia/Photo Researchers, Inc., 32
© Tom McHugh/Photo Researchers, Inc., 42
National Archives, 61
© Glenn Oliver/Visuals Unlimited, 7
PhotoDisc, 11, 15, 16, 25, 26, 36, 39, 45, 55
Reuters/Ho/Archive Photos, 8
St. Mary's Hospital Medical School/Science Photo
    Library/Photo Researchers, Inc., 22
© SIU/Visuals Unlimited, 28
Andy Walker, Midland Fertility Services/Science Photo
    Library/Photo Researchers, Inc., 79

About the Author

Jeanne DuPrau is a writer, teacher, and editor who lives in California. She has written a book about adoption and a book about meditation, as well as many essays and articles on a variety of subjects, including computers, natural science, and history.